Object Orientation

in

Visual FoxPro®

Object Orientation in Visual FoxPro®

Savannah Brentnall

With a foreword by Ken Levy

Addison-Wesley Developers Press

Reading, Massachusetts • Menlo Park, California • New York
Don Mills, Ontario • Harlow, England • Amsterdam
Bonn • Sydney • Singapore • Tokyo • Madrid • San Juan
Paris • Seoul • Milan • Mexico City • Taipei

Library of Congress Cataloging-in-Publication Data

Brentnall, Savannah.
    Object orientation in Visual FoxPro / Savannah Brentnall.
      p.   cm.
    Includes bibliographical references
    ISBN 0-201-47943-5
    1. Object-oriented programming (Computer science) 2. Visual
FoxPro for Windows. I. Title.
QA76.64.B7 1996   96-1313
005.75'65–dc20   CIP

Sponsoring Editor: Kathleen Tibbetts
Project Manager: Sarah Weaver
Production Coordinators: Erin Sweeney and Deborah McKenna
Cartoons: Suzanne Nielsen
Cover design: Chris St. Cyr
Set in 10 point Boom Light by Kim Arney, Pure Imaging

1 2 3 4 5 6 7 8 9 -MA- 0099989796
First printing, March 1996

Addison-Wesley books are available for bulk purchases by corporations, institutions, and other organizations. For more information please contact the Corporate, Government, and Special Sales Department at (800) 238-9682.

Find A-W Developers Press on the World-Wide Web at:
http://www.aw.com/devpress/

Contents

Chapter 8:

The Object-Oriented Development Team. 157

Appendix A:

Glossary of Terms 173

Appendix B:

Bibliography 185

Index. 191

Foreword

I met Savannah in October of 1992 at the first Xbase X3J19 ANSI committee meeting at the Jet Propulsion Laboratory (JPL) in Pasadena, California. I was then working for a company in the Los Angeles area that created public safety dispatch systems, and it was my first visit to JPL. Savannah and I didn't converse much, and all I remember about her was that she was the only one at the meeting with hair longer than mine.

We next met in June of 1993 at Leonard Zerman's summer solstice party. At this point, I was working at JPL. I didn't recognize Savannah at first, because her hair was now shorter than mine. In a group discussion, she started talking about something called object-oriented programming, about which I had read only briefly at the time. I asked her if she was interested in coming out to JPL to do research in object-oriented programming. Two months later, she was working there full-time.

While I was developing tools in FoxPro, Savannah became my OOP mentor and kept me on the right track as I pursued my research on books and products on object-oriented technology. The more I worked with OOP, the more I realized that object-oriented technology was going to hit us like a tidal wave, and we had a choice of catching a good ride or getting nailed in the sand.

There are many ways to interpret the various books and materials on OOP, and different authors sometimes have unique ways of describing the terminology. The two things I remember most about learning object-oriented technology are that it took patience and persistence. It's not like the early days when you could pick up Tom Rettig's *Handbook for FoxPro 1.0* and read through it in a weekend knowing all four corners of FoxPro, then later use the book as a great reference. Object orientation is a technology that is continuously evolving, and there are no walls or corners. OOP developers need to continuously research, study, have an open mind, and practice, practice, practice. Savannah uses great analogies and real-world examples to clarify the terminology, benefits, and pitfalls in making the transition from procedural programming to OOP. The key benefits of OOP are increased reusability, improved maintenance, and of course, more fun. The more effort you put into the discipline of making the paradigm shift to the OO world, the bigger the payoff for your investment. Now I can't imagine programming in a development environment that doesn't support OO.

Savannah's knowledge and enthusiasm for teaching OOP classes are conveyed in the text and illustrations found in *Object Orientation in Visual FoxPro*. There are basically two major steps in learning how to design and create OOP software. The first step is to obtain a clear understanding of the techniques and terminology associated with OO analysis and design. Although the actual coding implementation is sometimes considered the easy part of OO systems, Savannah takes the sting out of the learning curve by using clear and accurate definitions. The second step is to take that knowledge and use it with a development tool that supports OOP to create components and applications.

What Savannah has done in *Object Orientation in Visual FoxPro* is to help get you over those initial hurdles in a clear and concise way. If you treat FoxPro as a religion (as I do), then *Object Orientation in Visual FoxPro* will become your bible. Let Savannah become your virtual OOP mentor. I'm sure you will enjoy this E ticket ride into the world of objects and classes.

Ken Levy

Acknowledgments

Many people have influenced the development of this book. I'd particularly like to thank Rich McConnell for patiently answering my many questions on object orientation since I first began working with the technology in 1989. Thanks also to Y. Alan Griver for all his help and encouragement, and to Ken Levy for getting me mixed up in this whole crazy FoxPro community in the first place! To Kathleen Tibbetts, Sarah Weaver, and the staff at Addison-Wesley: Thanks for being such a joy to work with. Finally, to Paul: Persistence is everything. Thanks for not giving up.

About the Author

Savannah Brentnall is an independent consultant specializing in object orientation and Lotus Notes. She is the coauthor of *The Visual Guide to Visual FoxPro* by Ventana Press and is currently working with Flash Creative Management to provide object orientation training to FoxPro developers.

Savannah is a consultant to the Jet Propulsion Laboratory and to Countrywide Funding Corporation. She was the editor of Pinnacle Publishing's *VO Developer* and *Reference Clipper* newsletters. Her articles have appeared in *VO Developer*, *Reference Clipper*, and *Data Based Advisor*, and she has spoken at conferences and user groups around the world. Savannah was previously CA's Clipper Product Champion and Nantucket's Technical Marketing Manager.

Savannah has been programming since 1985 and has worked with object-oriented languages since 1989. She has been working as a Lotus Notes developer and administrator since the product first entered beta testing in 1989.

Savannah is available for writing, training, and development projects involving object orientation and Lotus Notes. She can be reached at the following numbers:

Telephone:　　(818) 841-7307

CompuServe:　　71024,3374

Internet:　　71024.3374@compuserve.com

Introduction

While much has been written on the subject of object orientation, many books devoted to the subject tend to either deal only with graphical objects such as forms and controls, or to talk about the entire subject as though it's something only rocket scientists can understand. Hopefully, this book falls somewhere between these two extremes.

This book is intended for programmers who have little or no experience in object orientation. It explains the terms and concepts of object orientation in a clear, concise way. While it is possible to write Visual FoxPro applications without using anything other than the built-in forms and controls, the real power of the language can be harnessed only by understanding how to subclass those built-in features and take advantage of Visual FoxPro's new object-oriented language.

The first chapters of this book begin with an explanation of fundamental terms and concepts. We then move on to discuss containership, data environments, object databases, analysis and design, and the roles in an object-oriented development team. By the time you finish reading, you should be ready to go forth and tackle object-oriented development in Visual FoxPro!

1

Benefits and Goals of Object Orientation

A physician, a civil engineer, and a computer scientist were arguing about which was the oldest profession in the world. The physician remarked, "Well, in the Bible, it says that God created Eve from a rib taken out of Adam. This clearly required surgery, so I can rightly claim that mine is the oldest profession in the world." The civil engineer interrupted, and said, "But even earlier in the book of Genesis, it states that God created the order of the heavens and the earth out of the chaos. This was the first and certainly the most spectacular application of civil engineering. Therefore, fair doctor, you are wrong: mine is the oldest profession in the world." The computer scientist leaned back in her chair, smiled, and then said confidently, "Ah, but who do you think created the chaos?"[1]

Chaos reigns in the world of computer science. Specifications that seemed hard and fast change, applications that were completed suddenly become inadequate for the job, and new technology makes the old solutions look primitive. Unless guidelines are established on how to anticipate and plan for this constant change, the ensuing chaos can be overwhelming.

Object orientation has become popular in the last few years partly due to the ease with which it enables applications to

---

1. From Grady Booch's *Object-Oriented Design with Applications*. (See Appendix B.)

survive this constant change. In this chapter, we'll look more closely at the benefits that this new paradigm brings.

Why Object Orientation?

We all know about the application backlog suffered by so many companies today. In some companies, it's so bad that users don't even bother to ask for new or improved applications because they know that it's unlikely the MIS department will be able to fulfill the request. Obviously there's a need for some form of software development that cuts down the amount of time it takes to create an application.

Increasingly, applications are being forced to deal with very complex data types. Industries like computer-aided design, engineering, and manufacturing have already run up against the limits of traditional systems architectures. Add to that the advancing popularity of multimedia systems, and you can see that traditional record- and file-based systems just aren't enough anymore. Waiting for language vendors to add new data types to those currently supported is not an ideal solution, either. It would be much easier if we were allowed to define our own data types, and that's really what we're doing when we add classes to an object-oriented application. We are defining how the data will be stored and the operations that can be performed on it.

Event-driven programming is being used in more and more systems, and it's almost impossible to do without objects. Imagine every window on the screen keeping track of its own coordinates, the data it's displaying, the databases it has open, and so on. How would you do that in a procedural environment? Call the window subroutine over and over again? How would you keep track of the contents of the variables? They'd be different in each iteration of the window. Maybe you could create a database and add records on the fly for each window or you could macro-create variables based on some unique naming scheme, but you can imagine how slow that would be—and kludgy, too. The most logical way to handle the problem is to use window objects.

So we have a need to quickly develop applications for all kinds of data types, including those that we ourselves define for particular applications. Well, that's exactly what object orientation is supposed to do.

The Benefits

The benefits of object-oriented programming aren't all that different from the benefits of good modular programming—they're just intensified. Faster development, easier maintenance, higher quality, and increased adaptability are all reasons why object orientation is being adopted throughout the industry. So let's look at how objects give you these advantages.

Faster Development

Faster development is something that comes once you've developed a library of reusable classes. Admittedly, developing these classes may take a little while, but the overall savings are worth it. In an insurance system of mine, it took some time to develop classes such as Insurer, Policy, and Ledger, and I threw away several early designs. However, I now have a set of classes that I can reuse over and over in future systems for this client.

You may be thinking that this class library seems just like a function library. In some ways, it is. The code is tested and can be used over and over again. The difference is in the way the two libraries are used. A function library vendor generally does not provide source code so you can't modify the functions in any way. And even if source is supplied, your modifications will be difficult to integrate with future versions of the library. A class library allows you to subclass the library's classes and adapt them in any way you like. You don't have to modify the class library itself; inheritance allows you to create a subclass and program only the differences.

This also applies to third-party libraries. Instead of being limited to the functionality that the library vendor provides, you can create your own subclasses and make the necessary modifications. Now that Visual FoxPro has been released, we should see an explosion in the number of available class libraries.

Easier Maintenance

Easier maintenance is a result of the encapsulation inherent in object-oriented systems. We all *try* to keep our modules self-contained when using procedural programming techniques, but object orientation enforces this. For example, I recently needed to change the structure of a database used to store insurance policies when most of the system had already been written. In a procedural system, I would have had to search for all the places in which the database was used and change those routines. This would have affected data entry screens, reports, browses— all kinds of things. In my object-oriented system, however, I only needed to change one class, the Policy class, because no other reports, browses, or other tasks explicitly use the Policy database—they simply ask a Policy object to supply them with data.

Higher Quality and Increased Adaptability

Ideally you can pull most of your application together from class libraries, which have already been tested and are known to be of high quality. This, combined with the ability to subclass existing classes and change behaviors without breaking existing code, results in higher quality systems that are easier to adapt to new uses.

Caveat

Remember that to achieve the benefits we just talked about, it isn't enough just to switch to an object-oriented language. You can use C++ to write C code, but what's the point? You have to follow the entire methodology. If you're not totally committed, the project's bound to fail.

The Downsides

Now that you've heard the benefits, what about the negatives? Well, obviously, there are some. The following sections list some of the major downsides to object orientation and suggest ways around them.

The Learning Curve

People have probably told you that to learn object-oriented programming you'll have to throw away everything you already know and start from scratch. Well, don't believe it. The people who tell you that are those who know object orientation is the way software is going and want to keep all the juicy work for themselves!

Of course, object orientation has a learning curve, just as every new technology does. Remember how freaked out people were by the Designer when it was first introduced to FoxPro? It's natural to be nervous and skeptical about change, especially if what you're doing now seems to work. But what works now may not be working best, or it may not work in the future.

If you're practicing good modular programming techniques such as information hiding, encapsulation, and so on, you may not find the switch to object orientation as hard as you expect it to be. Many people find it to be more of a switch in viewpoint. Instead of thinking about routines that act on data, try thinking about routines that ask the data to perform a task.

For example, in my insurance system, I switched from having detailed New Policy, Edit Policy, Delete Policy, and Policy Report routines, and I created a Policy class that contained Display, Edit, Delete, and Print methods. Now the New Policy menu option simply creates a policy object and asks it to edit and save itself. In addition, I now have a reusable Policy class that accurately models how this insurance company treats policies. I can use this class over and over again in future systems that I may write for them.

Execution Speed

Opponents of object technology will tell you, "Well, it's a nice idea, but it's too slow to work in the real world." It's true that the speed of some object-oriented languages is not as great as that of, say, Visual FoxPro, but there are slow procedural languages, too! Languages like Visual FoxPro and C++ offer object orientation without slowing down execution.

Where Do I Start?

The best way to decide whether object orientation will work for you is to try it on a pilot project. I know that that's sometimes hard to do as developers—every hour we're not working for a client is one we can't bill for—but it's worth it in the long run.

Don't follow the traditional approach of picking a problem and coding a solution from scratch. Instead, pick an area of your business—say, billing—and build a set of classes that models the way it works. Build account classes, invoice classes, and so on. Don't try to write an application yet.

Once you've built your classes, decide what your application is going to do and write it using the classes you've already created. Maybe you could start with time recording and billing. Then use the same classes to write another application, say, an accounts ledger program.

The reason for conducting the experiment this way is that it reflects the way object-oriented applications are created. You don't typically start from scratch; instead, you start with a set of classes that model the way a particular business works. Those classes are used over and over again in different applications, which leads to an overall increase in development speed.

Summary

In this chapter, we've looked at some of the benefits of object orientation, and some of the often-cited downsides. Before we move to the meat of the technology (in other words, the terminology and concepts), let's look at where this "object stuff" came from.

2

Origins of Object Orientation

Although object orientation appears to be a relatively new technique, it has actually been in existence for several decades. The first language to make a major contribution to the evolution of object-oriented programming was LISP in the 1950s. In 1967, Simula 67 added the concepts of encapsulation and inheritance. However, the main force behind object orientation's development as a commercial language was the Smalltalk research project at the Xerox's Palo Alto Research Centre (PARC).

Smalltalk

Alan Kay, a graduate student at the University of Utah, realized that some of the concepts in Simula could enhance his graphics work. He joined Xerox in the early 1970s as the head of the Smalltalk project, the goal of which was to create a language that supported the concept of classes introduced by Simula and that included a graphical user interface that the user could directly manipulate. The language continued to be enhanced and eventually became Smalltalk-80, which was released in 1981. Xerox continued to promote object technology and even spun off a separate company called ParcPlace Systems to make Smalltalk more commercially accepted. The standard components of modern graphical user interfaces—such as windows, icons, and the mouse—were pioneered at Xerox PARC.

All subsequent object-oriented languages have been based on the concepts used in Smalltalk. Smalltalk is important not just for its language, but also for its environment. Its development tools include class browsers and object inspectors. (A class browser displays all the classes in a system in a graphical "tree" and allows you to use the mouse to select the class you want to view or edit.) Most tasks, such as the creation of new classes, are menu driven and are far less complex and tedious than in a traditional editing environment. Smalltalk has also largely influenced the look and feel of graphical user interfaces (GUIs) like the Macintosh, Motif, and Windows.

Until recently, there were two primary Smalltalk vendors: ParcPlace Systems (Smalltalk-80) and Digitalk (Smalltalk/V). Digitalk has become known for their PC-based implementations, whereas Smalltalk-80 remains particularly popular in academic and government circles. In 1995, ParcPlace Systems and Digitalk announced plans to merge their two companies to form ParcPlace-Digitalk and deliver a single, uniform version of Smalltalk. This should further increase Smalltalk's popularity for the development of business applications.

Despite this support, object orientation didn't really have an impact on commercial software development until recently. Procedural languages became very popular when object-oriented languages were still in the research laboratory. Only with the introduction of object extensions to C and Pascal has progress accelerated.

Object Pascal

Object Pascal was created by developers at Apple Computer, Inc., who worked in conjunction with Niklaus Wirth, the designer of Pascal. Object Pascal first became available in 1986 and was the first object-oriented language to be supported by the Macintosh Programmer's Workshop, the development environment for Mac computers.

Object Pascal was the inspiration for two other object-oriented versions of Pascal: Quick Pascal from Microsoft and Turbo Pascal from Borland. More recently, Object Pascal served as a model for Borland's new Delphi language.

C++

C++ was developed by Bjarne Stroustrup at AT&T in the early 1980s. It added polymorphism and inheritance to C's speed and efficiency. Version 2.0 of C++ added multiple inheritance, among other things.

C++'s rise in popularity has been mainly due to its performance; code produced in C++ is almost as fast as code produced with regular C compilers. And the recent release of visual programming tools such as Microsoft's Visual C++ has made what was traditionally seen as a hard-to-learn language seem much more attractive.

Pure versus Hybrid Languages

The introduction of languages like C++ and Object Pascal has split the supporters of object technology into two camps. One camp supports the "pure" object-oriented languages such as Smalltalk and Actor, where everything is an object. For example, to add two numbers together in Smalltalk, you must create two integer objects, and send an Add message to the first one with the second being passed as a parameter.

The other camp prefers the "hybrid" languages such as Visual Objects, Visual dBASE, C++, Object Pascal, Objective-C, and CLOS. A hybrid language adds object-oriented extensions to an existing procedural language, and it is to this group that Visual FoxPro belongs.

On the whole, the pure languages emphasize development techniques such as rapid prototyping, where an application evolves from the interaction of the client, the programmer, and a prototype system. They are especially useful in cases where the client isn't exactly sure how the system should work, but can gradually refine the requirements as a result of working with a prototype. Pure object-oriented languages are also useful learning environments, because the rules are consistently enforced.

Hybrid systems emphasize runtime speed and the ease with which a procedural programmer can incorporate object-oriented extensions. Robust class libraries and large toolsets have traditionally been found in the purer languages, but they are beginning to be incorporated in the hybrids.

The downside of hybrid languages is that they allow developers to bypass the features of object orientation and continue coding in a procedural style. Because the rules of object orientation are not strictly enforced as they are in a pure language like Smalltalk, developers often end up creating code that is a mixture of object-oriented and procedural techniques and thus is hard to maintain. Even more important than the consideration of object orientation versus procedural is the fact that the development team follow one cohesive methodology throughout.

Visual FoxPro combines the best elements of both pure and hybrid languages. Its rich array of tools allows rapid prototyping and easy upsizing of local data, whereas its hybrid approach to object orientation allows developers to make use of their existing Xbase knowledge. It does, however, fall prey to the hybrid downside of failure to enforce strict object orientation. That leaves it up to us as developers to enforce those methods in our teams.

Summary

So that's the history lesson. You know now where object orientation came from and who some of the major contributors to its continued evolution were. But what does that have to do with FoxPro developers? Why is object orientation suddenly so important to us? Well, to answer that question, let's look at some of the concepts and see how they benefit application developers.

3

Terminology and Concepts

The terminology associated with object orientation may seem confusing at first. Why do we need terms like "class" and "method" when "function" has always done the job perfectly well in the past? The reason is that the job has changed somewhat. Instead of calling a *function* to perform a task on some data, we ask the data to perform that task on itself, using whatever *method* that *class* of data normally uses. Clear as mud? Well, read on . . .

Classes

A class is a template that describes all the attributes (*properties*) and behaviors (*methods*) of a particular type of data. (I know. You've heard that definition before. But it really is the best way to describe a class.) For example, a class called Box would probably contain information on the coordinates of a box and the characters used for its outline, and it would contain code for all box operations such as Show, Hide, Move, Resize, and so on. For example:

```
1. DEFINE CLASS Box AS Custom
2.    nTop     = 0
3.    nLeft    = 0
4.    nBottom  = 0
5.    nRight   = 0
```

```
 6.    cOutline = "/-\|/-\|"
 7.
 8. FUNCTION Init
 9.    <Initialize object>
10. RETURN this
11.
12. FUNCTION Show
13.    @ this.nTop, this.nLeft, this.nBottom, this.nRight BOX cOutline
14. RETURN this
15.
16. ENDDEFINE
```

Remember that a class is just a template. It doesn't actually perform any operations; it merely describes how they should be performed. To actually store data and act upon it, you need an object. You may find it helpful to think of a class as a "cookie cutter" that manufactures objects. This is shown in Figure 3–1.

Figure 3–1. *A class is a "cookie cutter."*

Objects

An object is an *instance* of a class. That's why the process of creating an object is known as *instantiation*—we're creating an instance of a class. For example, Box is a class, but you need to create a Box object in order to use the methods defined in that class.

The following code creates a Box object (an instance of the Box class) from the class shown in the previous section:

```
oBox = CreateObject( "Box" )
```

This code asks the Box class to create a new instance of itself. A reference to this new object is then assigned to the oBox memory variable. It's important to note that oBox is just a regular memory variable and can be local, public, or private. The only thing special about it is that the data it contains isn't of type character, numeric, and so on, but is of type "object reference."

> ❖ **Note:** Before you can create an object, you must first SET PROCEDURE TO the appropriate file, in the case of hand-coded classes, or SET CLASSLIB TO in the case of visual classes stored in .VCX files (these are explained later).

Constructors

Whenever an object is created from a class, a method called a *constructor* is executed. This simply adds the appropriate properties to the object and optionally assigns initial values to those properties. In Visual FoxPro, the constructor is not a separate routine; rather, it is the code that appears between the DEFINE

CLASS statement and the first method. For example, in the following piece of code, the constructor appears in italic:

```
1. DEFINE CLASS Box AS Custom
2.    nTop     = 0
3.    nLeft    = 0
4.    nBottom  = 0
5.    nRight   = 0
6.    cOutline = "/-\|/-\|"
7.
8. FUNCTION Show
```

As its name suggests, a constructor is a piece of code that actually constructs an object and adds properties like nTop, nLeft, and so on. All properties must be listed in the constructor, or they will not become part of the object. If you don't want to assign values yet, assign values of .NULL., as follows:

```
1. DEFINE CLASS Box AS Custom
2.    nTop     = .NULL.
3.    nLeft    = .NULL.
4.    nBottom  = .NULL.
5.    nRight   = .NULL.
6.    cOutline = "/-\|/-\|"
7.
8. FUNCTION Show
```

Some languages (like C++) allow you to define multiple constructors, each with difference sets of parameters. This is known as *constructor overloading*. The constructor called when an object is created depends on the number of parameters passed. This facility is not available in Visual FoxPro; however, you can simulate it by allowing multiple parameters to be passed and checking them on receipt in the constructor.

Initializers

To assign initial values to an object, we use an *initializer*. In Visual FoxPro, this is an optional routine that is always called Init. It is invoked automatically when an object is created, immediately following the execution of the constructor. For example,

```
1. FUNCTION Init
2.    this.nTop    = 0
3.    this.nLeft   = 0
4.    this.nBottom = 0
5.    this.nRight  = 0
6.    this.cOutline = "|/-\|/-\"
7. RETURN this
```

You may have noticed that these assignments look the same as the ones we previously placed in the constructor. In fact, they are. If the initialization process is as simple as setting initial values of some properties, you can place the initialization code immediately following the DEFINE CLASS line. However, sometimes you may want to perform more complex processing in the initializer. Let's develop the Box initializer a little further, and enable it to take parameters, as follows:

```
1. FUNCTION Init( top, left, bottom, right )
2.    this.nTop    = IIf( Empty(top),    0, top )
3.    this.nLeft   = IIf( Empty(left),   0, left )
4.    this.nBottom = IIf( Empty(bottom), 0, bottom )
5.    this.nRight  = IIf( Empty(right),  0, right )
6.    this.cOutline = "|/-\|/-\"
7. RETURN this
```

This initializer accepts the coordinates of the box as optional parameters. If none are passed, the coordinates default to zero. The passing of parameters to an initializer is entirely optional.

In this case, it makes sense because it is impossible to have a box that doesn't have coordinates. The initializer parameters are passed using the following syntax:

```
oBox = CreateObject( "Box", 10, 10, 20, 35 )
```

TIP: Generally, values that are essential to an object are passed as parameters. For example, you can't use a database table without knowing its name, so the Name property should be passed as a parameter to a DbfTable initializer.

Notice that the initializers in these examples always return a value of this. Although we won't fully discuss the this keyword until later in this chapter, what's important to understand here is that any value other than .F. is permissible. Returning .F. causes the object creation process to fail, and no object is created.

The initializers we've looked at so far have been fairly simple. However, an initializer can call UDFs, open tables, and do anything else that has to be done in order to initialize an object.

TIP: Some languages roll the constructor and initializer into one routine, usually called Init. Hence, you may sometimes see the Init routine referred to as a constructor.

Destructors

As its name suggests, a *destructor* is a method that is called whenever an object is killed or released from memory, either by the system's virtual memory manager or by the programmer. A destructor allows you to put "clean up" code into a class. Destructors are often used to perform functions like reclaiming memory or rolling back partially completed database transactions. (See Figure 3–2.)

The destructor in Visual FoxPro is called Destroy and is triggered automatically in response to a Destroy event. However, you can also call it directly whenever you need to. Simply call the Destroy routine, and then release the memory variable contain-

Figure 3–2. *A destructor allows an object one last chance to execute instructions.*

ing a reference to the object in question. Here's an example of a Destroy routine.

```
 1. *           Class: Customer
 2. *            Name: Destroy()
 3. *     Description: Destructor routine
 4. *-------------------------------------------------------------
 5. *      Arguments: None
 6. * Return Value: this
 7. *-------------------------------------------------------------
 8.
 9. FUNCTION Destroy
10.     LOCAL nAnswer
11.
12.     * Make sure customer has been saved
13.     IF .NOT. this.lSaved
14.        nAnswer = MessageBox("This customer has not been saved. " + ;
15.           "Save now?", 4 )
16.
17.        IF nAnswer == 6        && "Yes"
18.           this.Save()
19.        ENDIF
20.
21.     ENDIF
22.
23.     this.Close
24.
25. RETURN this
```

This example allows you to save the current Customer object before it's released. This should not replace good error handling in the application itself, however. Instead, this is a "safety net"—a last-ditch attempt to catch errors that may not have been caught thus far. Developers often put code in a destructor to handle errors that should never occur during normal use.

❖ ***Note:*** It's important to note that although the destructor can be used to clean up before an object is released, you cannot prevent the destruction once the Destroy routine has begun execution.

Properties (Instance Variables)

A *property*, sometimes known in object orientation terms as an *instance variable,* is simply a variable used to store data in an object. The name "instance variable" is derived from the fact that an object is an *instance* of a class, and the object's data is stored in a *variable.*

A property is accessed by sending a message to the object. The following example uses a Box object's cOutline property:

```
1. oBox = CreateObject( "Box", 10, 10, 20, 35 )
2.
3. * Ask the Box object for the value of its cOutline property
4. ? oBox.cOutline      && Displays "|/-\|/-\"
5.
6. * Assign a new value to the cOutline property
7. oBox.cOutline = "|/=\|/=\"
8.
9. ? oBox.cOutline      && Displays "|/=\|/=\"
```

To look at the property values for a particular object, you can use the property sheet in the graphical tools described later in this book. However, it's often useful while debugging to create an object in the Command window and use the DISPLAY OBJECTS command to show its property values.

Methods

A *method* is a piece of code that performs an action with an object's data and is invoked by sending a message to an object.

Within a class, a method of that class is invoked by sending a message to this (discussed later in this chapter). For example,

```
1. oBox = CreateObject( "Box", 10, 10, 20, 35 )
2.
3. * Send a Show message to the oBox object, asking it
4. * to invoke the Show method in the Box class
5. oBox.Show()
```

As you read this book, you may notice that some examples place parentheses after the name of the method. This is not necessary unless you intend to store the method's return value. For example,

```
1. oBox.Hide              && This is OK
2. lHideOK = oBox.Hide    && This won't work
3. lHideOK = oBox.Hide()  && This will
```

Although the parentheses are unnecessary in some circumstances, many programmers prefer to use them all the time in order to create uniformity in their code. I recommend using them to help you distinguish between properties and methods.

 TIP: It is permissible to have methods with the same names as regular procedures or functions. Visual FoxPro knows which to execute based on the calling syntax you use.

Visual FoxPro provides three ways to add a method:

1. Hand-coding the method between the DEFINE CLASS and ENDDEFINE statements in the .PRG file.

2. Using the New Property/Method option on the Class menu in the Class Designer.

3. Using the New Property/Method option in the Form Designer (for visual objects).

There is one important caveat about using the third option. You are adding the method code to an individual object, not to the class definition for that object. This means that other objects created from the same class will not be able to execute the new method. As a general rule, it's better to add method code to the class definition rather than to individual objects.

Event Methods

In Visual FoxPro, an *event method* is a method that is called automatically whenever a particular event occurs. We've seen two examples already:

1. The Init method is called whenever an object is initialized (an Init event).

2. Destroy method is called whenever an object is released (a Destroy event).

Some people use the terms *event* and *method* interchangeably. In actual fact, they are different, although they often work hand in hand. When an event occurs, Visual FoxPro automatically executes a method with the same name. So if the event was called MouseUp, FoxPro looks for a method called MouseUp.

Note that although you can call event methods directly in your code just like other methods, you cannot trigger their related events. For example, you can call the Destroy method, but you cannot cause a Destroy event to occur. A Destroy event can only occur when an object is destroyed. In reality, this is not usually a problem; however, it does mean that you cannot programmatically simulate events occurring. In other words, you can call your own methods, but you cannot do whatever Visual FoxPro might be doing in addition to calling your methods, such as garbage collection and the actual release of the object's memory space.

The Visual FoxPro events shown in Table 3–1 apply to objects created from most of the built-in classes.

Note that in form objects, the Load method is called *before* the Init method. Conversely the Unload method executes after the Destroy method.

Table 3–1. *Typical Visual FoxPro Events*

Event	Triggered When...
Load	A form or formset is loaded into memory.
Unload	A form or formset is released from memory.
Init	An object is created.
Destroy	An object is destroyed.
Click	The user clicks on the object.
DblClick	The user double-clicks on the object.
RightClick	The user right-clicks on the object.
GotFocus	The object receives focus.
LostFocus	The object loses focus.
KeyPress	The user presses a key.
MouseDown	The user presses a mouse button while the mouse pointer is over the object.
MouseMove	The user moves the mouse over the object.
MouseUp	The user releases the mouse button while the mouse pointer is over the object.
InteractiveChange	Any of the object's properties are changed interactively.
ProgrammaticChange	Any of the object's properties are changed programmatically.

Messages

In order to invoke a method (function) or query an object's data, a *message* must be sent to the object. A message usually consists of the name of the object (known as the *receiver*), followed by the name of a property or a method that the object knows how to execute, followed by any parameters. For example, the message to display a box might look as shown in Figure 3–3.

The diagram in Figure 3–3 is described as "sending a Show message to oBox." The effect of this message is to invoke the Show method for the oBox object and to pass .T. as a parameter. In case you're wondering, the period (.) is known as the *member access* or *dot operator*. It simply tells Visual FoxPro to send the message on the right to the object on the left, and it is equivalent to the colon used by other languages such as Smalltalk and Visual Objects.

The example in Figure 3-4 assumes that the Show method shown earlier has been amended to accept a logical parameter.

Consider the following code example.

```
1. cOutline = "/-\|/-\|"
2. cText    = "Text in a box"
3. =ShowBox( 10, 10, 22, 78, cText, cOutline, .T. )
```

In the preceding example, a traditional function is used to display a piece of text centered in a box. This function would probably be stored in a function library. Compare that with the

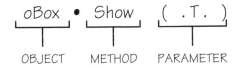

Figure 3–3. *The structure of a message.*

Figure 3–4. *We communicate with an object by sending it messages.*

following example where a Show message is sent to a TextBox object:

```
1. oTextBox = CreateObject("TextBox", 10, 10, 22, 78 )
2.
3. oTextBox.cContents = "Text in a box"
4. oTextBox.cOutline  = "|/-\|/-\|"
5. oTextBox.lCenter   = .T.
6.
7. oTextBox.Show()
```

Although these two examples are functionally equivalent, they serve to illustrate the syntactical differences between procedural code and object-oriented code.

The New Message

Many object-oriented languages send a New message to a class in order to create an object. This automatically invokes the constructor method for an object of that class. As we've already seen, FoxPro uses the CreateObject() function to create objects. When you look at magazines that specialize in object orientation, a line such as this

```
oBox := Box.New( 10, 10, 20, 35 )
```

is equivalent to FoxPro's

```
oBox = CreateObject( "Box", 10, 10, 20, 35 )
```

TIP: Because many object-oriented languages use the New message, it's a good idea to avoid using it in your own Visual FoxPro classes. That way, programmers with experience in other object-oriented languages will have less of a learning curve when joining your team.

This

So far, all of our examples have sent messages to objects using the following syntax:

```
object.message
```

However, if you need to access an object from within one of its own methods, a slightly different syntax is used as follows:

```
this.message
```

This is shorthand for "send the message on the right to this object." In this context, "this object" is the object to which a message was sent in order to execute the current method. Some

object-oriented languages such as Smalltalk use "self" instead
of "this." Let's look at another example.

```
1. * Box.prg                        1. * String.prg
2. DEFINE CLASS Box AS Custom        2. DEFINE CLASS String AS Custom
3.    cOutline = "/-\|/-\|"          3.     cContents = ""
4.    nTop      = 0                  4.
5.    nLeft     = 0                  5.
6.    nBottom   = 0                  6.
7.    nLeft     = 0                  7.
8.                                   8.
9. FUNCTION Init( top, left, ;       9. FUNCTION Init( contents)
10.                                  10.
11.    bottom, right)                11.    <constructor code>
12.    <constructor code>            12. RETURN this
13. RETURN this                      13.
14.                                  14.
15. FUNCTION Show                    15. FUNCTION Show( nRow, nCol )
16.                                  16.
17.    @ this.nTop, this.nLeft,;     17.    @ nRow,nCol SAY this.cContents
18.    this.nBottom, this.nRight ;   18. RETURN this
19.    BOX this.cOutline             19.
20. RETURN this                      20.
21.                                  21.
22. ENDDEFINE                        22. ENDDEFINE
```

The following example uses these two classes:

```
1. oBox    = CreateObject( "Box", 10, 10, 20, 35 )
2. oString = CreateObject( "String", "Savannah" )
3.
4. * Inside this Show method, this = oBox
5. oBox.Show()
6.
7. * Inside this Show method, this = oString
8. oString.Show( 22,10 )
```

The `Show` method in the Box class needs coordinates in order to display the box. These coordinates are stored in the `nTop`, `nLeft`, `nBottom` and `nRight` properties. We've already said that you access a property by using the syntax `<object name>.<property name>`, but what object name can we use inside the `Show` method? `oBox` is a private variable, which means it's not visible inside the `Show` method. Besides, if you hard-coded references to `oBox` inside the `Show` method, everyone who used your Box class would have to call their Box objects `oBox`!

That's where the `this` keyword comes in. `this.nTop` means "the `nTop` property *in whatever object we're currently working with*." Because the `Show` method was executed by sending a message to `oBox`, this is effectively equal to `oBox`.

 TIP: The same message (`Show`) is being sent to objects of two different classes, with different results. This capability is called *polymorphism*, and is discussed later in this chapter.

Using This in Forms

Sometimes it's useful to be able to call a method or property of a particular form. For example, let's say you wanted to put an Exit button on a form. In order to close the form, you need to call the form's `Release` method. However, adding the line

```
this.Release()
```

to the button's `Click` method only calls the `Release` method in the button, not in the form. We need a generic way of saying: "Call a method in whatever form this control is on." That's where the thisForm keyword comes in. The code for the Click method in the button now looks like this:

```
thisForm.Release()
```

If you want to refer to the formset that a form is a part of, use the thisFormSet keyword. This can be used inside any forms in the set and in any controls on those forms.

 TIP: The this, thisForm, and thisFormSet keywords are only used inside methods. Using these keywords anywhere else will result in an error.

Returning This

You may have noticed that several of the examples presented so far return a value of this. This is customary in object-oriented languages when no specific value needs to be returned. Returning this allows you to combine more than one message. For example,

```
oBox.Show().SetFocus()
```

Since the Show method returns this (a Box object), you can send the SetFocus message directly to Show's return value.

Visual FoxPro does not yet support this "chaining" of message sends. Instead, you can send multiple messages to the same object using the folowing syntax:

```
1. WITH oBox
2.         .Show()
3.         .SetFocus()
4. ENDWITH
```

Inheritance

So far, you may be wondering why there's so much fuss about object-oriented programming. Well, *inheritance* is one of the capabilities that makes object orientation so popular.

Imagine that you have a box class such as the one listed. It may even have been written by another programmer or be part of the company code library. Either way, it works and you don't want to mess with it. Unfortunately you need a box class that asks the user a question and waits for a Y or N response.

In a traditional application, you'd have to take one of two actions:

1. Modify the Box function to accept a logical parameter indicating whether or not to accept input from the user.

2. Copy the Box function, paste the code into a new function, and then make the necessary modifications.

There are problems with both these approaches. The first option asks you to modify an existing piece of code that is known to be free of problems and may be used in its current state by many other people. The second option forces you to maintain two nearly identical sets of source code.

In an object-oriented language, the answer is simple. You create a new class, YesNoBox, that inherits all the properties and methods of Box. YesNoBox can add properties and methods of its own and can modify and redefine those inherited from Box. For example,

```
1. DEFINE CLASS YesNoBox AS Box
2.    cContents = ""
```

```
 3.
 4. FUNCTION Show
 5.    LOCAL cAnswer
 6.    cAnswer = " "
 7.
 8.    * Call Show method in Box class.  This just displays the box
 9.    Box::Show()
10.
11.    * Get the user's response
12.    @ this.nBottom-1, this.nLeft + 2 SAY this.cContents;
13.       GET cAnswer PICTURE "Y"
14.    READ
15. RETURN cAnswer == "Y"
16.
17. ENDDEFINE
```

Now, I can display a Yes/No box using the following code:

```
1. oBox           = CreateObject( "YesNoBox", 10, 12, 20, 45 )
2. oBox.cContents = "Cannot open Customer file.  Continue (Y/N)?"
3. lContinue      = oBox.Show()
```

In this example, the Box class is known as the *superclass*. The YesNoBox class is known as the *subclass*. (See Figure 3–5.) The line Box::Show() uses FoxPro's *scope resolution operator* (::) to send a message directly to the Box class. The reason for this is that the Box class contains a perfectly good routine to display a box on the screen. Even though we're going to ask the user for input, we need to display the box first. Instead of rewriting all that code, why not just call the Show method in the Box class?

❖ **Note:** Most books and articles on object orientation use the industry-standard term *superclass*. However, Visual FoxPro uses *parent class* instead (not to be confused with *parent objects* or *parent containers*!). In addition, the term *base class* is generally used to refer to the class at the base of the class tree. Visual FoxPro uses

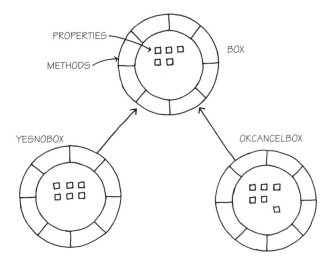

Figure 3–5. *Each subclass is a more specialized version of the superclass.*

the term to refer to the built-in classes that are provided with the product.

Calling Methods in the Superclass

Many object-oriented languages use the keyword *super* to send a message to the superclass. Because Visual FoxPro does not support this keyword, we have used the scope resolution operator, as explained in the preceding section. However, there is an alternative. Every class can respond to the message parentClass. This returns the name of the superclass. You can then add the name of the method you wish to execute and Eval( ) the whole expression, as follows:

```
=Eval( this.parentClass + "::Show()" )
```

This example also calls the Show method in the Box class because Box is the superclass of YesNoBox.

You could use Visual FoxPro's #define directive to make this code a little easier to understand. For example, placing the directive

```
#define super.     Box::
```

at the top of the file containing the Box class definition would allow you to say super.Show() throughout your Box class code.

 TIP: The SuperCls utility automates this process and provides a toolbar that you can use to insert messages to superclasses. SuperCls is provided with the *Codebook* (see Appendix B) and is also available for downloading from the FOXUSER forum on CompuServe.

Chaining Initializers

It makes good sense for the Init method in a class to initialize only the properties that were defined in that class. (See Figure 3–6.) Otherwise, each successive subclass would have longer and longer Init methods! However, because methods redefined in a subclass override any methods of the same name in the superclass, you must manually chain together the Init methods.

For example, if we had an initializer in the YesNoBox class, we'd have to add a call to the Box initializer to complete the process, like this:

```
1. * In the YesNoBox class:
2. FUNCTION Init
3.    <Do YesNoBox initialization>
4.    =Eval( this.parentClass + "::Init()" )
5. RETURN this
```

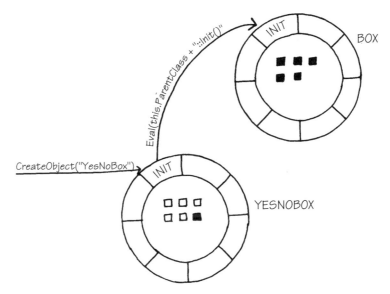

Figure 3–6. *Each* Init *method initializes only the properties for its class.*

This is very important, because failure to call the Init method in the superclass could cause the inherited properties to have incorrect values.

Dealing with Unwanted Properties in the Subclass

When you inherit from a class, you automatically inherit all the properties of the original class. These properties cannot be deleted, which is an important point to remember when dealing with form classes.

When you create a form, add controls, and save the form as a class, the controls become properties of the form class you've created. If you then subclass the class, the controls are inherited. *This means they cannot be deleted.* If you open the subclass in the Class Designer and try to delete any of the inherited controls, Visual FoxPro says that it "Cannot delete objects because some are members of a parent class."

 TIP: Because an inherited control cannot be deleted from a form class, set the Visible property to .F. to make the control "disappear." To make the control "invisible" in design mode as well, set the Top and Left properties to –100.

Understanding the Property Sheet

Whenever you right-click on an object in the Form Designer or the Class Designer, a shortcut menu appears. From this menu, you can use the **Properties** option to show the property sheet for this object. (Alternatively, choose the **Properties** option on the View menu.) The screenshot in Figure 3–7 shows the property sheet for the TSMainForm class in the Tasmanian Traders sample application.

The BaseClass property shows the name of the built-in Visual FoxPro class on which this class was originally based, no matter how far up the hierarchy. The Class property shows the name of this class, and the ParentClass property shows the name of its superclass. The Name property shows the name of a particular object, as opposed to the name of its class.

Multiple Inheritance

So far, we've only talked about subclasses inheriting from a single superclass. However, some products allow a subclass to inherit from multiple superclasses. This is known as *multiple*

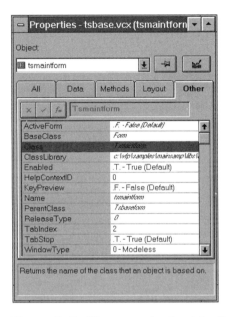

Figure 3–7. *The property sheet for the TSMainForm class.*

inheritance. Visual FoxPro does not support multiple inheritance, and as I'm about to explain, this is not a serious flaw in the language.

The use of multiple inheritance adds a number of complex problems to system design. The first problem is one of *name clashing*. If you're inheriting from two classes that both contain a method with the same name, which one do you execute? The second problem involves passing messages up to a superclass. If there are five superclasses, which one does the message go to? And finally, there's the issue of design. Use of single inheritance produces a fairly easy-to-understand class diagram that looks similar to a family tree. Multiple inheritance, on the other hand, tends to produce a design that more closely resembles a plate of spaghetti!

TIP: In general, many people use multiple inheritance to work around earlier design problems. It is usually possible to avoid multiple inheritance by using delegation and container classes, which are explained later.

The use of multiple inheritance is still the subject of much debate in object orientation circles. Many people believe that it adds an unnecessary layer of complexity to a system, without a corresponding gain in functionality.

Hierarchies

Most people envision classes and subclasses as a kind of tree diagram. In fact, the organization of the classes in a system is usually referred to as a *class tree* or *class hierarchy*. This hierarchy can grow quite large as a system develops, and several tools have been developed to make it easier to represent this hierarchy as a diagram.

Many object-oriented languages, such as Smalltalk, incorporate a graphical *browser*, which shows the classes in a tree format. The Professional Edition of Visual FoxPro also includes a Class Browser, which shows each class in either alphabetical or hierarchical format, and displays the properties and methods of each class. The Visual FoxPro Class Browser is covered in Chapter 5.

Finding Methods and Variables in a Hierarchy

When an object receives a message, it looks in its class definition for a corresponding method or property. If no match is found, the request is passed "up the tree" to its superclass (see Figure 3–8).

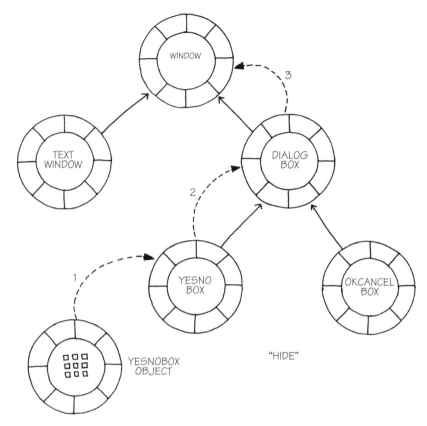

Figure 3-8. *Searching for the* Hide *method.*

This process continues until the method or property is found. If the object gets to the top of the class hierarchy and still hasn't found a match, an error is displayed.

Because it can take time to scan the entire hierarchy, object-oriented systems can be slower than their procedural counterparts. However, this is becoming less and less of an issue as object-oriented languages evolve and become faster. Yes, passing a message in this manner may be nanoseconds slower than calling a function directly, but the gains in code maintainability and reuse far outweigh this.

TIP: Don't be tempted to use the scope resolution operator to force Visual FoxPro to search in a specific class for a property or method: it ties those classes together and reduces flexibility.

Preventing Message Sends for Nonexistent Properties and Methods

As was mentioned in the previous section, if a message reaches the top of the class hierarchy without finding a matching method or property, an error message is displayed. But wouldn't it be a better idea to prevent the sending of messages for which there is no corresponding method or property? This is where the AMembers() function comes in. AMembers() returns an array containing the names of all the properties and methods for a specified object. For example,

```
 1. FUNCTION IsAvailable( oObject, cName )
 2.    LOCAL ARRAY aArray[1]
 3.    LOCAL lFound
 4.
 5.    * Create array of properties and methods for oObject
 6.    =AMembers( aArray, oObject, 1 )
 7.
 8.    * Is cName in this list?
 9.    lFound = ( AScan( aArray, Upper(cName) ) <> 0 )
10. RETURN ( lFound )
```

The IsAvailable function checks to see whether a specified method or property name is valid for a specified object. Ideally IsAvailable would be a method in each of your own classes. However, if this requires too much code duplication because your classes don't all have a common superclass, it's acceptable to make it a standalone function.

TIP: Because the AMembers() function capitalizes the names of the properties and methods in the array, it's important that you use the Upper() function to put the message name you're searching for in uppercase.

In this example, the AMembers() function has been used with the number 1 as a parameter. This tells Visual FoxPro to include the names of all methods and properties. In fact, FoxPro actually creates a two-dimensional array, with the second column indicating whether the item in the first column is a property or an array. If you specify AMembers() without the third parameter, Visual FoxPro defaults to providing a one-dimensional array containing only the names of the properties. Passing 2 as the third parameter tells Visual FoxPro to create a list of all the member objects that this object contains (container objects are explained in Chapter 4).

TIP: I recommend that in your IsAvailable() function, you use 1 as the third parameter to AMembers() because it returns both properties and methods.

The Visual FoxPro Class Hierarchy

Visual FoxPro comes with built-in classes. As mentioned earlier, the FoxPro documentation refers to them as base classes. Table 3–2 lists the built-in classes.

The classes in italic are nonvisual classes, meaning that they can be used programmatically, but don't refer to visual screen elements such as buttons and edit controls.

Table 3–2. *Visual FoxPro Built-in Classes*

Controls	Containers
CheckBox	Container
ComboBox	*FormSet*
CommandButton	Form
Control	Grid
Custom	Column
EditBox	*PageFrame*
Header	Page
Image	Toolbar
Label	OptionButtonGroup
Line	CommandButtonGroup
ListBox	
OLEBoundControl	
OLEContainerControl	
Shape	
Spinner	
TextBox	
Timer	

Polymorphism

Polymorphism is the ability to send the same message (such as Show) to objects of different classes and have each object respond in its own way. (See Figure 3–9.) Although this can be mimicked without object orientation, the code tends to become unmanageable.

Consider the following example of a generic DisplayData procedure:

```
1. cString = "This is a string"
2. =Show( cString, 10, 10 )
3.
4. nNumber = 135
5. =Show( nNumber, 10, 10 )
6.
```

Figure 3–9. *Sending the same message to different objects can cause different actions.*

```
 7. dDate   = CToD( "05/05/93" )
 8. =Show( dDate, 10, 10 )
 9.
10.
11. PROCEDURE DisplayData( xItem, nRow, nCol )
12.     DO CASE
13.     CASE Type( "xItem" ) == "C"
14.         @ nRow,nCol SAY xItem
15.
16.     CASE Type( "xItem" ) == "N"
17.         @ nRow,nCol SAY Str( xItem )
18.
19.     CASE Type( "xItem" ) == "D"
20.         @ nRow,nCol SAY DToC( xItem )
21.     ENDCASE
22. ENDPROC
```

It's convenient to be able to use the same function name for displaying different types of data, but FoxPro reports a naming conflict if you do that. The only solution, without object orientation, is to create a single function that contains a CASE statement to handle every possible data type. As you can imagine, that quickly becomes cumbersome. Not only that, but the code must be modified every time a new data type is added to the language.

When you're using an object-oriented language, however, each class can have its own Show method. You no longer have to concern yourself with naming conflicts. An added advantage is that you can create classes that are completely self-contained, or *encapsulated*. In an object-oriented language, the preceding example would look like this:

```
1. oString = CreateObject( "String", "This is a string" )
2. =DisplayData( oString )
3.
4. oNumber = CreateObject( "Number", 135 )
```

```
 5. =DisplayData( oNumber )
 6.
 7. oDate   = CreateObject( "Date", CToD( "05/05/93" ) )
 8. =DisplayData( oDate )
 9.
10. DEFINE CLASS String AS Custom
11.     <properties>
12. FUNCTION Show
13.     <show code>
14. RETURN this
15. ENDDEFINE
16.
17. DEFINE CLASS Number AS Custom
18.     <properties>
19. FUNCTION Show
20.     <show code>
21. RETURN this
22. ENDDEFINE
23.
24.
25. DEFINE CLASS Date AS Custom
26.     <properties>
27. FUNCTION Show
28.     <show code>
29. RETURN this
30. ENDDEFINE
31.
32.
33. PROCEDURE DisplayData( oObject )
34.     oObject.Show()
35. ENDPROC
```

Whenever a new data type is added, we just need to add a new class for it, rather than modifying existing code.

Even though we don't know what type of object oObject is, we can send it a Show message. That's because Visual FoxPro "stamps" each object with the name of its class (in the Class property) when the object is first created. So oObject "knows" which class it was created from. Visual FoxPro goes to this class to find a Show method, and continues up the hierarchy as explained earlier in this chapter.

Encapsulation

Encapsulation is the building of self-contained, "black box" code. In traditional Xbase programming, it means creating functions that don't rely on the values of variables defined in higher level routines, and explicitly passing to those functions all the data they need to in order to operate.

In an object-oriented language, an encapsulated class is one that contains all the properties and methods it needs in order to complete its task. It should contain its own Show, Hide, Edit, and Save methods, for example, instead of calling routines from a common library.

An encapsulated class is also one that hides its implementation from "outsiders." For example,

```
1.  * Wrong:
2.  oCustManager = CreateObject( "CustManager" )
3.  nOldArea     = Select()
4.  oCustManager.Browse()
5.  SELECT ( nOldArea )
6.
7.  * Right:
8.  oCustManager = CreateObject( "CustManager" )
9.  oCustManager.Browse()
10.
11. * In CustManager class:
12. FUNCTION Browse
13.    LOCAL nOldArea
```

```
14.    nOldArea = Select()
15.    .
16.    . <Select new workarea and do browse>
17.    .
18.    SELECT ( nOldArea )
19. RETURN this
```

In lines one to six the calling routine is forced to save the current workarea before sending a Browse message to the CustManager object. This is incorrect—a well-designed CustManager class should save the state of the environment on entry and restore it upon returning. As the user of the CustManager class, you shouldn't have to concern yourself with implementation details such as whether or not the Browse method saves the current workarea first.

 TIP: Encapsulation is similar to the principle of information hiding that was a cornerstone of traditional structured programming. Object-oriented languages simply enforce this principle rather than leaving it up to individual programmers to implement.

Encapsulation not only protects an object's data from corruption by outside sources, but it also protects other objects from relying on an object's internal structure. If a Customer class is properly encapsulated, for example, we can change the way it calculates its outstanding invoice amount by changing just one piece of code: the Customer class itself. Other objects continue to ask a Customer object to calculate the amount as usual—they don't care that the internal process has changed.

Summary

In this chapter, you've learned some of the basic terms and concepts of object-oriented programming. By now, you should understand what a class is and how it's used, and how Visual FoxPro handles objects when messages are sent to them. In Chapter 4, we'll continue on this theoretical bent with some more advanced concepts.

4

Further Concepts

Container (Composite) Objects

Some objects have characteristics that are too complex to be stored as simple numbers or text strings. For example, a Company class has a contact person as one of its characteristics, but that contact person has characteristics and functions of its own. In an object-oriented language, this would be represented by a *container object* (known in other languages as a *composite* or *aggregate object*).

A container object is one that contains one or more other objects. This means that we can create a Contact class that describes the characteristics and behaviors of a contact at a company, and we can include an object of that class inside our Company class (see Figure 4–1).

Visual FoxPro's use of the word "container" is contrary to usual object orientation terminology, which uses "container" to mean a special kind of composite object—one in which every property is another object. A good example of a traditional container is an array. In Visual FoxPro, a container object is also known as the *parent*. If it contains controls, those controls are referred to as *child controls*.

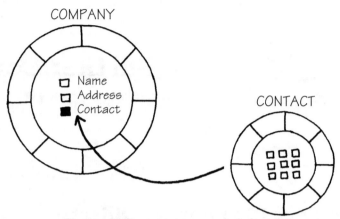

Figure 4–1. *A container object.*

The relationship between a *container* object and the objects "inside" it (known as *member objects* or *object members*) is known as *containership, composition,* or *aggregation,* and it is an example of collaboration between two classes. In fact, classes can collaborate in several ways; this particular example is known as either an "is-part-of" or a "has" relationship. Class relationships are described in more detail in Chapter 7.

Table 4–1 lists the built-in Visual FoxPro container classes, together with the types of objects they can contain.

Let's look at a source code example. The following code shows a piece of the class definition for a basic Company class:

```
1. DEFINE CLASS Company AS Container
2.
3.    lNew      = ""    && Is this a new company?
4.    cName     = ""    && Name of company
5.    cMail1    = ""    && Mailing address
6.    cMail2    = ""
7.    cMail3    = ""
```

Table 4–1. *Visual FoxPro "Container" Classes and Their Contents*

Container	Contents
CommandButtonGroup	Command buttons
Container	Any objects
Control	Any controls
Custom	Any objects
FormSet	Forms and toolbars
Form	PageFrames, any controls, containers, and custom objects
Column	Column headers, any objects except forms, formSets, columns, and toolbars
Grid	Columns
OptionButtonGroup	Option buttons
PageFrame	Pages
Page	Any controls, containers, and custom objects
Toolbar	Any controls, pageFrames, and containers

```
 8.    cMail4      = ""
 9.    cMailState  = ""
10.    cMailZip    = ""
11.    cOther1     = ""        && Other address
12.    cOther2     = ""
13.    cOther3     = ""
14.    cOther4     = ""
15.    cOtherState = ""
16.    cOtherZip   = ""
17.    cPhone      = ""        && Phonc number
18.    c800Phone   = ""        && 800 number
19.    cFax        = ""        && Fax number
20.
21.    ADD OBJECT oContact AS Contact   && Contact object for this class
```

Line 21 shows the definition of a property called oContact. This is a Contact object that represents the contact person for this customer. Because the Company class may be used in many different applications, it makes sense to incorporate the Contact object as part of the class definition. Because oContact is an object that is a member of the Company class, it is often referred to as a *member object*.

The ADD OBJECT command can only be used in the construction code for a class. It performs the following tasks:

1. Create a property with the specified name (for example, oContact) and add it to the class definition.

2. Instantiate the contained class.

3. Store the resulting object in the specified property (oContact).

To further set up this Contact object, we could change line 21 as follows:

```
1. * Set up Contact object
2. ADD OBJECT oContact AS Contact;
3.    WITH cName = "", lNew = .T.
```

This revision adds the Contact object and sets the values of its cName and lNew properties to an empty string and to .T., respectively. You can initialize as many properties as you want in this way; just separate them with commas.

As was mentioned in Chapter 3, the DISPLAY OBJECTS command can be used to display the value of an object's properties. Figure 4–2 shows the property values for a Company object. Note the reference to the oContact object member. Since the Company object contains a Contact object, we call it a container object, created from a container class.

```
       LEFT                      N    0              (      0.00000000)
       LNEW                      C    ""
       MOUSEPOINTER              N    0              (      0.00000000)
       NAME                      C    "Company1"
       PARENTCLASS               C    "Container"
       PICTURE                   C    ""
       SPECIALEFFECT             N    2              (      2.00000000)
       TABINDEX                  N    0              (      0.00000000)
       TABSTOP                   L    .T.
       TOP                       N    0              (      0.00000000)
       VISIBLE                   L    .T.
       WIDTH                     N    200            (    200.00000000)

Member Objects:
       OCONTACT          CONTACT

Methods and Events:
       ADDOBJECT                 CLICK                    DBLCLICK
       DESTROY                   DRAG                     DRAGDROP
       DRAGOVER                  DRAW                     ERROR
       GOTFOCUS                  INIT                     LOSTFOCUS
       MOUSEDOWN                 MOUSEMOVE                MOUSEUP
       MOVE                      MOVED                    REFRESH
       REMOVEOBJECT              RESIZE                   SAVEASCLASS
       SETALL                    SETFOCUS                 UIENABLE
       ZORDER
```

Figure 4–2. *The DISPLAY OBJECTS command showing a Company object.*

More About ADD OBJECT

When the ADD OBJECT line in the example in the preceding section is executed, Visual FoxPro calls the Init method in the Contact class. As was mentioned earlier, whenever an Init method returns false (.F.), the object is not created. When the object in question is a composite object, the failure of Init methods in any of the added objects also causes the creation process to fail.

It is possible to avoid calling the Init method in the member object. To do this, simply add the NOINIT clause after the ADD OBJECT command as follows:

```
ADD OBJECT oContact AS Contact NOINIT
```

This creates the Contact object and assigns it to the oContact property without calling the Init method in the Contact class. However, the constructor code in the Contact class is still executed.

TIP: The ADD OBJECT command can only be used inside the constructor. If you try to use it anywhere else, Visual FoxPro issues an error.

ADD OBJECT versus CreateObject()

You may be wondering why I'm using the ADD OBJECT command instead of the CreateObject() function. CreateObject() simply creates an object, whereas ADD OBJECT creates an object and adds a property of that name to the current class. For example,

```
1. DEFINE CLASS Company AS Container
2.    <properties>
3.
4. FUNCTION Init
5.    * This creates a Contact object, and stores it in a
6.    * memvar called oContact.
7.    oContact = CreateObject( "Contact" )
8. RETURN this
9.
10. ENDDEFINE
```

If I then instantiate this Company class and attempt to query the Contact's name, like this

```
1. oCust = CreateObject( "Company" )
2. ? oCust.oContact.cName
```

I get the error shown in Figure 4–3 because oContact is just a memory variable, rather than a property of the Company class.

ADD OBJECT versus the AddObject Method

Whereas the ADD OBJECT command is used inside class definitions to add object members, the AddObject method (which is

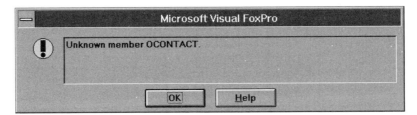

Figure 4–3. *The error that results from trying to access a nonexistent property.*

defined in the Container base class) is designed to add objects to a container *at runtime*. In most cases, I recommend that you build object members into the class definition instead of allowing them to be added willy-nilly at runtime. That way, it's clear to users of the class exactly what they're supposed to add.

Avoiding Cyclical Constructor Calls

When you use the ADD OBJECT command to add an object to a class, Visual FoxPro calls the object's constructor at runtime. What happens if that constructor contains an ADD OBJECT command to add an object of the original type? Consider this example:

```
 1. * Company class
 2. DEFINE CLASS Company AS Container
 3.    ADD OBJECT oContact AS Contact
 4.    <code>
 5. ENDDEFINE
 6.
 7. * Contact class
 8. DEFINE CLASS Contact AS Container
 9.    ADD OBJECT oCompany AS Company
10.    <code>
11. ENDDEFINE
```

If I try to create a Company object, the Company class calls the constructor for the Contact class. The ADD OBJECT command in the Contact class calls the constructor in the Company class, and so on. We've created a recursive constructor call and will eventually run out of stack space. Adding the NOINIT clause only prevents execution of the Init method, not the constructor itself.

The class design in the preceding example is perfectly valid. A Company class could contain the name of the contact at that company, and a Contact class could contain the company where the person works. To break the recursion cycle, one of the classes must use CreateObject() instead of ADD OBJECT, like this:

```
1. * Company class
2. DEFINE CLASS Company AS Container
3.     oContact = .NULL.
4.
5. FUNCTION Init
6.     this.oContact = CreateObject( "Contact" )
7.
8.
9. * Contact class
10. DEFINE CLASS Contact AS Container
11.     ADD OBJECT oCompany AS Company NOINIT
12.     <code>
13. ENDDEFINE
```

Here, the oContact property has been added in the constructor, but it is assigned a .NULL. value. We assign it a reference to a Contact object in the initializer. For this to work, the NOINIT clause must be added to the ADD OBJECT command in the definition of the Contact class.

There is one problem with this technique. It requires that you know the implementation of each class in order to use either of them. If someone working on the Company class in the future were to revert to the ADD OBJECT command, the Contact class would also be affected. This is not ideal because it limits the flexibility of both classes. It would be better to assign .NULL. as the initial value in both classes, but this leads us back to the cyclical constructor problem, as you can see from the following example:

```
 1. * Company class
 2. DEFINE CLASS Company AS Container
 3.    oContact = .NULL.
 4.
 5. FUNCTION Init
 6.    this.oContact = CreateObject( "Contact" )
 7. RETURN this
 8.
 9. ENDDEFINE
10.
11.
12. * Contact class
13. DEFINE CLASS Contact AS Container
14.    oCompany = .NULL.
15.
16. FUNCTION Init
17.    this.oCompany = CreateObject( "Company" )
18. RETURN this
19.
20. ENDDEFINE
```

In this example, creating a Company object executes the Init method in the Company class. That, in turn, creates a Contact object, which executes the Init method in the Contact class. That creates a Company object, and so on. All we've done is move the problem from the constructor to the Init method. Because there's no NOINIT clause with the CreateObject() function, there's no way to resolve the problem using this syntax.

To resolve the problem entirely, we must remove the instantiation process from methods such as Init, over which we have limited control. To do this, we have to add methods such as AddCompany and AddContact. For example,

```
1.  * Company class
2.  DEFINE CLASS Company AS Container
3.     oContact = .NULL.
4.
5.  FUNCTION AddContact
6.     this.oContact = CreateObject( "Contact" )
7.  RETURN this
8.
9.  ENDDEFINE
10.
11.
12. * Contact class
13. DEFINE CLASS Contact AS Container
14.    oCompany = .NULL.
15.
16. FUNCTION AddCompany
17.    this.oCompany = CreateObject( "Company" )
18. RETURN this
19.
20. ENDDEFINE
```

 TIP: Use ADD OBJECT to add simple objects such as controls. Use the technique described here when adding objects that are themselves containers.

Delegation

If we create an object called oCompany from the Company class shown in the preceding section, and we want to call our contact at this company, we have to say:

```
oCompany.oContact.Call()
```

This forces us to know the internal implementation of the Company class; namely, that the contact information is stored in a property called oContact and that the oContact object can respond to a Call message. If the person who wrote the Company class then changes the property name, we have to change all our code. Not only that, but we're being forced to communicate not just with the object we've created, but directly with the objects that it contains.

Many container classes contain two-line methods that simply pass a message along to the object contained in one of their properties. For example, the CallContact method for the Company class shown in the preceding section might look like this:

```
1. FUNCTION CallContact
2.     this.oContact.Call()
3. RETURN this
```

This is known as *delegation* or *message forwarding*, because we're delegating responsibility for the task to another class and forwarding the message to another object. (See Figure 4–4.)

Creating a method like CallContact means that we only have to communicate with the Company object itself. Now, we can call the contact person by writing this:

```
oCompany.CallContact()
```

Some languages allow us to specify delegation in the class definition. We can then replace the CallContact method with:

```
MESSAGE CallContact IS Call TO oContact
```

This means "whenever you are sent the CallContact message, send a Call message to the oContact property." This is much easier to read and doesn't clutter up the rest of the source code with two-line methods. However, Visual FoxPro does not yet support this syntax.

Figure 4–4. *Delegation or message forwarding.*

Scoping

Scoping is usually split into two parts: visibility and lifetime. *Visibility* refers to the places in which the variable can be accessed, and *lifetime* describes the amount of time for which it exists.

There are several types of scoping options for memory variables: public, private, and local. Table 4–1 gives an overview of the different scopes available in Visual FoxPro.

Scoping of Properties and Methods

When we use the term "scope," most of us think of memory variables. However, scoping is not limited to variables and func-

Table 4-1. *Variable Scopes in Visual FoxPro*

Scoping Option	Visibility	Lifetime
Public	Entire application	Entire application
Private	Creator routine and its subroutines	Creator routine and its subroutines
Local	Creator routine	Creator routine and its subroutines

tions. Most object-oriented languages also allow scoping control over the properties and methods of a class. The available scopes are listed in Table 4–2.

❖ **Note:** The hidden scope is not yet supported in Visual FoxPro. However, its use is explained here in order to give a full description of the scopes commonly available in object-oriented languages and because it is likely to be supported in the future.

Scoping of Properties

A class defines not only the properties and methods that an object will have, but also the scope of those properties and

Table 4-2. *Scoping for Properties and Methods in Visual FoxPro*

Scope	Visibility and Lifetime
Exported	Entire application
Protected	Creator class and its subclasses
Hidden	*Creator class only*

methods. Paying careful attention to scoping can help you design classes that will survive future enhancement without having to be completely rewritten. The following sections look at the scoping options available in Visual FoxPro.

Exported Scope

When a property is defined as *exported* (*public* in C++), it is accessible outside the class in which it was defined. This is the default for Visual FoxPro properties and doesn't require any special keywords. Consider the following segment of the class definition for Company:

```
1.  DEFINE CLASS Company AS Container
2.
3.      lNew        = ""
4.      cName       = ""
5.      cMail1      = ""
6.      cMail2      = ""
7.      cMail3      = ""
8.      cMail4      = ""
9.      cMailState  = ""
10.     cMailZip    = ""
```

All of these properties are exported, which means that they can be directly manipulated by any part of the system that has a reference to a Company object. For most properties, this is sufficient. It certainly makes sense to export such basic company information as name, address, and so on. However, there are times when you want to prevent properties from being changed outside of the class.

Protected Scope

Protected properties (same in C++) are similar to exported properties, except that they are only visible to the class in which they're defined and its subclasses. In the preceding class definition for the Company class, lNew is a flag that tells me whether or not this is a new company. This flag is set to True (.T.) in the Init method, but it is immediately set to False (.F.) the moment the object is filled with company information from a database table or is saved to a table. We may wish to make lNew a protected property because changing its value alters whether or not a new record is appended when the information is saved.

```
 1. DEFINE CLASS Company AS Container
 2.
 3. PROTECTED lNew
 4.    lNew = .T.    && Is this a new company?
 5.
 6.    cName      = ""
 7.    cMail1     = ""
 8.    cMail2     = ""
 9.    cMail3     = ""
10.    cMail4     = ""
11.    cMailState = ""
12.    cMailZip   = ""
13.
14. ENDDEFINE
```

Now, lNew can't be accessed except by one of the methods in the Company class, or in a method in one of Company's subclasses. This means that the following code will return an error:

```
1. oCompany = CreateObject("Company")
2. ? oCompany.lNew       && Error--lNew doesn't exist
```

❖ **Note:** Visual FoxPro does not allow the scope of a property to be changed in a subclass. Therefore, lNew will always be a protected property.

Hidden Scope

Properties that are defined as *hidden* (*private* in C++) can only be accessed from within methods inside the class itself. You'll get an error message if you try to access them from outside the class definition.

Another important feature of hidden properties is that they are not accessible in subclasses. This is particularly important for commercial class libraries where vendors want to ensure that customers cannot fundamentally change the workings of a class by subclassing and altering important properties or methods.

Scoping of Methods

Most object-oriented languages also allow for the scoping of methods in the same fashion as properties, and Visual FoxPro is no exception. In fact, the lack of method scoping should be considered a fairly serious flaw in an object-oriented language. Let's take another look at our Company class.

```
1. DEFINE CLASS Company AS Container
2.
3. PROTECTED lNew
4.     lNew       = .T.     && Is this a new company?
5.
6.     cName      = ""
7.     cMail1     = ""
8.     cMail2     = ""
9.     cMail3     = ""
10.    cMail4     = ""
11.    cMailState = ""
12.    cMailZip   = ""
13.
```

```
14. PROTECTED FUNCTION GetLineItems
15.    <code>
16. RETURN this
17.
18. FUNCTION InvoiceClient
19.    <code>
20. RETURN this
21.
22. ENDDEFINE
```

The InvoiceClient method can be called anywhere. The GetLineItems method, which is called from the InvoiceClient method, cannot be called from outside the Company class or one of Company's subclasses. This is because GetLineItems is just one part of a larger process that creates an invoice for a client.

You can use the PROTECTED keyword to restrict access to any methods that are used for internal processing in the class.

The Benefits of Scoping in Classes

There are several advantages to restricting the information that is available about a class. First of all, it ensures that people using that class only know what they need to know, and nothing more. The interface is small and clean, which fulfills another of those traditional structured programming principles: small interfaces.

Protecting properties and methods also means that we can change their internal implementation without breaking other people's code. For example, we can change the code in GetLineItems without worrying because we know that nobody is able to access it directly.

The Public Interface to a Class

The public interface to a class defines the protocol that you must follow in order to access an object of that class. All exported properties and methods are part of the public interface. It's similar to an API (Application Programming Interface), in that it allows people to use a class and be sure that they won't have to change their code later, even if the internals of the class change.

It's important to design your classes so that the public interface is resistant to change. After all, by exporting methods and properties, you're telling other programmers that it's all right to go ahead and use them. If you then change the names of those properties or the return values of the methods, you're not going to be a popular person! Imagine how upset you'd be if you used a Microsoft API in one of your applications, only to find that the function names all changed in the next release of the API. Think of the public interfaces to your classes in the same way.

We have seen how using scoping in properties and methods can help define the public interface to an object. Let's now look at other techniques that can help refine the public interface.

❖ **Note:** Access methods, assign methods, and calculated properties are not currently supported in Visual FoxPro. However, their usefulness and widespread acceptance in object-oriented languages makes it likely that they will be implemented in a future version.

Access and Assign Methods

As mentioned earlier, protected properties are not directly accessible from outside a class definition. To access these properties, you must use an exported method. This creates an inconsistency in that some properties can be accessed in the usual way as follows:

```
object.property = 1
```

and some only via methods:

```
object.SetProperty( 1 )
```

Another alternative is to use *access* and *assign* methods. As their names suggest, these kinds of methods are called automatically whenever a property is accessed or assigned a value. The main advantage of access and assign methods is that the person using your class does not have to use a different syntax to manipulate properties for which access and assign methods have been defined.

> ❖ **Note:** Access and assign methods are not currently supported in Visual FoxPro. They are explained here to allow you to better understand code in magazines devoted to object technology, and because they are likely to be added to Visual FoxPro in the future.

Access and assign methods usually work as a pair. Their most basic use is to provide access to protected properties in a controlled manner. For example:

```
1. * Description: Simple rectangle
2. *  Superclass: Custom
3. *-----------------------------------------------------------------
4.
5. DEFINE CLASS Rectangle AS Custom
6.
7.    PROTECTED nLength, nWidth
8.       nLength = 0
9.       nWidth  = 0
```

```
10.
11. ACCESS FUNCTION nLength
12. RETURN this.nLength
13.
14. ASSIGN FUNCTION nLength( length )
15.     this.nLength = length
16. RETURN this.nLength
17.
18. ENDDEFINE
```

The access method for nLength shown in the preceding example could be executed by the following code:

```
? oRect.nLength
```

The assign method would be executed if the following code occurred:

```
oRect.nLength = 10
```

In this case, the value 10 would be passed as a parameter to the assign method for nLength.

The advantage of access and assign methods is that the code executed when a property is manipulated can be changed at any time, without affecting the code that uses the class.

In some cases, validation must be performed before an assignment can be completed. Without access and assign methods, we have only three ways of doing this:

1. Force the class user to perform the assignment via an exported method.

2. Force the class user to call a validation method.

3. Leave validation entirely up to the class user.

None of these validation methods is particularly appropriate. With access and assign methods, however, validation can be performed automatically and transparently whenever necessary. For example, let's make sure that negative values can't be assigned to the nLength property. Note in the following example that we haven't had to change any of the calling code in order to add this validation:

```
1. *           Name: nLength
2. *          Class: Rectangle
3. *    Description: Assign method for nLength
4. *      Arguments: length - New length
5. * Return Value: this.nLength
6. *------------------------------------------------------------
7.
8. ASSIGN FUNCTION nLength( length )
9.
10.    IF length > 0
11.       this.nLength = length
12.    ELSE
13.       WAIT WINDOW "Cannot assign negative number to nLength"
14.    ENDIF
15.
16. RETURN this.nLength
```

Let's say that we want to create a TextInBox class that can dynamically change the size of a box when its contents expand or shrink, depending on the setting of an AutoSize flag. Here's the class definition:

```
1. * Description: Box with text inside
2. *  Superclass: Box
3. *------------------------------------------------------------
4.
5. DEFINE CLASS TextInBox AS Box
6.
```

```
 7.     lAutoSize = .T.
 8.     cContents = ""
 9.
10. ENDDEFINE
```

Remember that the Box class contains properties for the coordinates, so we don't have to redefine them here. We're simply adding new properties, cContents and lAutoSize, to hold the box contents and the AutoSize indicator.

If we're going to modify the size of the box whenever the contents change, we need access and assign methods for cContents.

```
 1. *           Name: cContents
 2. *          Class: TextInBox
 3. *    Description: Access method for cContents
 4. *      Arguments: None
 5. * Return Value: this.cContents
 6. *-----------------------------------------------------------------
 7.
 8. ACCESS FUNCTION cContents
 9. RETURN this.cContents
```

```
 1. *           Name: cContents
 2. *          Class: TextInBox
 3. *    Description: Assign method for cContents
 4. *      Arguments: cNewValue - New text
 5. * Return Value: this.cContents
 6. *-----------------------------------------------------------------
 7.
 8. ASSIGN FUNCTION cContents( cNewValue )
 9.    LOCAL nDifference
10.
11.    * Make sure this is a character value
12.    IF Type( "cNewValue" ) <> "C"
13.       WAIT WINDOW "Cannot assign non-character value to cContents"
14.       RETURN( this.cContents )
```

```
15.    ENDIF
16.
17.    * Make sure text isn't more than 74 characters
18.    IF Len( cNewValue ) > 74
19.       WAIT WINDOW "Cannot assign text greater than 74 characters"
20.       RETURN( this.cContents )
21.    ENDIF
22.
23.    nDifference    = Len( cNewValue ) - Len( this.cContents )
24.    this.cContents = cNewValue
25.
26.    * Only change coordinates if length of text has changed,
27.    * and if lAutoSize is .T.
28.    IF nDifference <> 0 .AND. this.lAutoSize
29.       this.nLeft  = this.nLeft  - Int( nDifference / 2 )
30.       this.nRight = this.nRight + Int( nDifference / 2 )
31.       this.Show()
32.    ENDIF
33.
34. RETURN this.cContents
```

Calculated Properties

It's also possible to use access methods to create *calculated properties,* which are properties that don't actually exist as properties in a class, but are accessed as though they do. In the preceding example, the Rectangle class has properties for length and width, but not for area. However, because it depends on the length and width, the area of a rectangle really should be calculated each time it's needed.

Despite this, the person using our Rectangle class shouldn't have to concern himself with the intricacies of our implementation. He should be able to ask for the area of a rectangle and receive a value. Because we don't want to store the rectangle's area, we create a calculated property to return the value, as follows:

```
1. *           Name: nArea
2. *          Class: Rectangle
3. *    Description: Access method for nArea
4. *      Arguments: None
5. * Return Value: this.nLength * this.nWidth
6. *-------------------------------------------------------------------
7.
8. ACCESS FUNCTION nArea
9. RETURN this.nLength * this.nWidth
```

This raises an interesting design issue. Should there also be a matching assign method for nArea? If so, what actions must it perform? If nArea equals nWidth multiplied by nLength, the following statements are also true:

1. nLength equals nArea divided by nWidth.

2. nWidth equals nArea divided by nLength.

Should the assign method for nArea update the nLength or nWidth properties? Exactly how this is implemented is a design decision. You may decide not to allow the area to be assigned, or you may decide to allow assignment and automatically adjust the length and width accordingly.

Let's look at a different example. Here, nRate is calculated each time it's needed. If we decide to store it as a property later, we can do so without affecting the code that uses this class.

```
1. * Description: Mortgage class
2. *  Superclass: Container
3. *-------------------------------------------------------------------
4.
```

```
 5. DEFINE CLASS Mortgage AS Container
 6.
 7. ACCESS FUNCTION nInterestRate
 8.    LOCAL nRate
 9.    nRate = <Calculation>
10. RETURN nRate
11.
12. ASSIGN FUNCTION nInterestRate( nRate )
13. RETURN .F.
14.
15. ENDDEFINE
```

 TIP: Access and assign methods should be used to provide a consistent interface to an object. They may also be used to perform range checking and to create calculated properties.

In these examples, I've used the same syntax regardless of whether I'm using exported properties or access and assign methods. However, not all languages allow this. It's definitely an advantage because it allows you to change between the two approaches without affecting the code that uses your class.

Generally access and assign methods are used for values that are not used often (why take up storage space when you only need a value at the end of each month?) or for values that must be calculated each time they're used. Access and assign methods are also used when validation must be done or when other data must be changed based on the value being assigned. Exported properties are used for values that are accessed often and for values that don't change often.

Class Libraries

As we develop more and more applications, we begin to build up a library of useful routines. Some companies maintain company-standard function libraries for all their developers to use. There are also many different third-party add-on libraries.

Most of us use at least one function library in our applications, and for good reason: They save time. Why waste time writing report routines when you can buy a reporting library that's already been tested and installed at hundreds of other companies?

The problem with traditional function libraries is that you're limited to what the vendor (or MIS department) provides. Many vendors do not provide source code for their libraries, which means you can't customize the code in any way. And even if source code is provided, the moment you modify it, you've made it impossible to upgrade to the next version of that library.

With class libraries, however, these problems are solved. To customize the code for your own uses, simply subclass the provided classes. You don't need to have the source code as long as you know the public interface to the class, and the message flow from class to class. Additional information can be retrieved if necessary by using the Class Browser, Class Designer, and DISPLAY OBJECTS command to examine the object's properties and methods.

Class libraries provide functionality for user interface design, financial algorithms, reporting, and many other categories. In fact, most object-oriented languages support a huge market of class libraries, in much the same way that FoxPro supports third-party function libraries.

Frameworks

Frameworks are class libraries that have been designed for particular business areas. They provide generic functionality upon which developers can build and from which subclasses can be created. Frameworks could be created for graphing, reporting, or user interface, for example. They could also be created for life insurance, sales tracking, or store inventory. Frameworks tend to be much more detailed and industry-specific than general-purpose class libraries.

When you're considering using a framework, be sure you choose carefully. Because your entire application is based on the classes provided by the framework, it's very hard to remove it later.

Frameworks whose purpose is to help developers build any application are known as *application frameworks*. These frameworks typically provide entities such as dialog boxes, container classes, and so on. However, the term is often used to apply to any framework. An application framework is a comprehensive set of classes that provides the basic functionality that is common to all applications.

Visual FoxPro comes with an application framework that allows you to create windows, menus, toolbars, and so on for your applications. To make our lives even easier, we can use visual tools to manipulate these elements, without having to write the code manually. In addition, the *Visual FoxPro Codebook* by

Y. Alan Griver (see Appendix B) is supplied with a new application framework that supplements the one supplied in Visual FoxPro.

Some of the advantages to using frameworks are the same as those of function libraries or third-party products:

- Using tried and tested code without the overhead of trying it and testing it yourself.

- Faster application development.

- Greater reusability.

Designing a Framework

We've already discussed the importance of designing a public interface to a class, however, the importance is even greater when designing a framework. When you distribute a framework, many developers use it as a basis for their class hierarchies and applications. Whenever you make any changes, they must at least recompile their classes. If you design the public interface carefully at the start, that's all they should have to do.

In addition to a carefully designed public interface, a framework needs excellent documentation. This should cover not only the classes and their purposes, but also the ways in which they interact. The aim is to provide enough information so that developers can to develop efficient subclasses, without revealing too much of the internal workings.

Wrapper Classes

To add new behavior to an existing class, the usual course of action is to subclass and make the necessary changes. However, in some cases that is not possible. For example, the old code may have been written in a procedural language such as FoxPro 2.6 or COBOL. You want to use the existing functionality as a base, but it isn't possible to subclass.

The solution is to create a wrapper class. Instead of calling the FoxPro 2.6 code directly, we "wrap" it inside a class. Of course, the 2.6 code is not actually contained within the class. It's just that the only way to access that code is through the wrapper class. The pseudocode would look something like this:

```
1. DEFINE CLASS MortgageInterest AS Custom
2.
3. FUNCTION Calculate
4.    <Save system state>
5.    <Call FoxPro 2.6 routine>
6.    <Restore system state>
7. RETURN this
8.
9. ENDDEFINE
```

 TIP: A good example of a wrapper class is found in the menu wrapper provided with the *Visual FoxPro Codebook.*

Drawbacks of Wrapper Classes

Many older routines are too large to reuse completely. Use of a wrapper class is a temporary measure that is intended to help bridge the gap between the old system and its object-oriented counterpart. Eventually it will be more efficient to rewrite the old code. In the meantime, the wrapper class provides an object-oriented interface to the older code. (See Figure 4–5.)

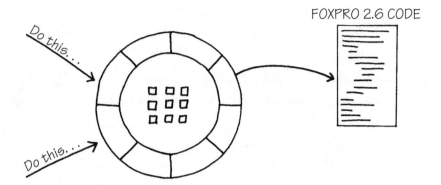

Figure 4–5. *A wrapper class provides an object-oriented interface to older code.*

Depending on the implementation, wrapper classes can be a little slower than regular code. For example, a wrapper class that has to use some kind of conversion utility to run a COBOL routine will probably be slower than the same routine rewritten from scratch. However, the wrapper class makes the migration possible while new solutions are being created.

Application Classes

Many designers use an *application class* to store the environment information for an application, launch menus and toolbars, and basically function as the "glue" that holds the application together. The Application class provided with Visual FoxPro is a good example. You can find it in VFP\SAMPLES\MAINSAMP\LIBS\TSGen.vcx. Here's the constructor:

```
1. **************************************************
2. *-- Class:      application (c:\vfp\samples\mainsamp\libs\tsgen.vcx)
3. *-- ParentClass:  custom
4. *-- BaseClass:    custom
```

```
 5. *-- Standard Application Class
 6. *
 7. #INCLUDE "c:\vfp\samples\mainsamp\include\tastrade.h"
 8. *
 9. DEFINE CLASS application AS custom
10.    Height = 34
11.    Width  = 92
12.
13.    *-- The caption of the main window for this application.
14.    cmainwindcaption = ""
15.
16.    *-- Name of main menu to run (.MPR file).
17.    PROTECTED cmainmenu
18.    cmainmenu = "MAIN.MPR"
19.
20.    *-- The name of the database to use for this application.
21.    PROTECTED cdatabase
22.    cdatabase = ""
23.
24.    *-- The name of the main window caption before this app started.
25.    PROTECTED coldwindcaption
26.    coldwindcaption = ""
27.
28.    *-- The number of form instances currently open.
29.    PROTECTED nforminstancecount
30.    nforminstancecount = 0
31.
32.    *-- A reference to the navigation toolbar.
33.    otoolbar = .NULL.
34.    Name = "application"
35.
36.    *-- Indicates if environment is "clean".
37.    PROTECTED lisclean
38.
39.    *-- Array of VFP toolbar names, and if they were open when the
40.    *-- application started.
41.    PROTECTED atoolbars[1,1]
42.
```

```
43.     *-- Contains form names, object references, number of current
44.     *-- running instances, and the next available instance number.
45.     DIMENSION ainstances[1,4]
```

The Do and DoMenu methods start the main menu, which controls the functionality of the application from that point on, as follows:

```
1. *-- Puts up the main menu and runs the application.
2. PROCEDURE Do
3.      *-- Put up main menu
4.      this.DoMenu()
5.
6.      *-- Start the event loop
7.      READ EVENTS
8. ENDPROC
```

```
1. *-- Puts up the main menu.
2. PROCEDURE domenu
3.      DO (this.cMainMenu)
4. ENDPROC
```

On Line 18 of the constructor, the Main.MNX menu was assigned to the cMainMenu property. As you can see from Figure 4–6, each option on this menu causes a form to be loaded or a particular toolbar button to be clicked.

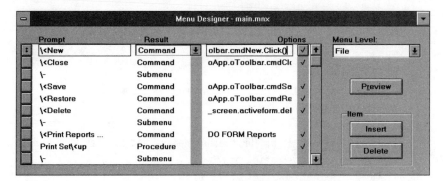

Figure 4–6. *The Menu Designer, showing Main.MNX.*

oApp is a public variable containing a reference to an Application object. Note that the Application class is fairly generic, and is intended to be subclassed for particular applications. This is known as an *abstract class*.

Summary

Well, that just about wraps up the discussion object-oriented programming terms and concepts. By now, you should be comfortable with even such advanced topics as delegation and containership. Enough theory! Let's take a look at the tools that make class creation and maintenance in Visual FoxPro so, well, *visual*.

5

The Visual Tools

One thing that distinguishes Visual FoxPro from its competitors is the ability to accomplish many programming tasks with graphical tools. The Class Browser and Class Designer allow you to create and manipulate classes without having to worry about .PRG files. This chapter examines the features of the Class Browser and Class Designer and shows you why Visual FoxPro lives up to its name!

The Class Browser

The Class Browser (shown in Figure 5–1) is the central tool in any object-oriented language. It allows you to view the class hierarchy and to easily see the methods and properties of the classes within that hierarchy.

The classes are shown in hierarchical or alphabetical order, depending on which of the boxes at the top of the browser have been checked. In hierarchical order, the class list functions as an outline, which means that you can collapse or expand a series of classes by clicking on the plus (+) and minus (-) symbols at the far left of the window.

A chevron (<<) beside the name of the class indicates that the superclass is contained in another class library. To add that class library to the browser display, double-click on the folder icon to the left of the chevron. The Class Browser not only adds

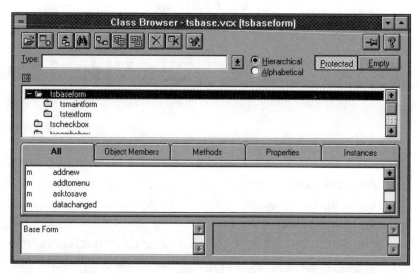

Figure 5–1. *The Class Browser.*

the additional library, but it also positions the highlight on the superclass of the class you selected.

As you highlight a class, its properties and methods are shown on the tabs at the bottom of the screen. These tabs are similar to those found in the Properties window of the other designers, with the addition of the **Object Members** and **Instances** tabs. The **Object Members** tab shows any objects that are a part of this class (that is, this class is a container class). For example, if we highlight the Company class described earlier in this book, oContact appears as an object member.

If you double-click on an object member, Visual FoxPro adds its class library to the browser (if necessary) and positions the highlight on the object member's class.

The **Instances** tab is useful when you're running the Class Browser while an application is executing. It shows you any current objects that have been created from the highlighted

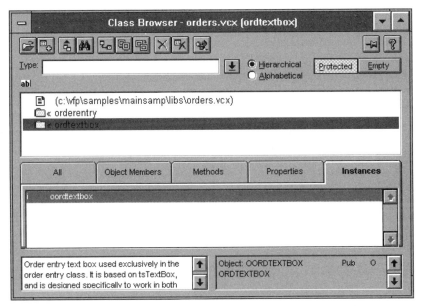

Figure 5-2. *The* **Instances** *tab showing an instance of OrdTextBox.*

class. Figure 5-2 shows the **Instances** tab with an instance of the OrdTextBox class highlighted. Notice the description in the right corner of the browser; in the case of an instance, it's the same as the result of the DISPLAY OBJECTS command.

At the bottom of the Class Browser are two description boxes. The left box shows the description of the class, and the right box shows a description of the currently highlighted method or property. These descriptions are added via the **New Property/ Method** or **Edit Property/Method** options on the Class Designer's Class menu, but they can also be edited directly in the Class Browser description boxes.

The **Protected** and **Empty** buttons are toggles that can be turned on or off. The **Protected** button toggles the display of protected properties and methods in the lower tabs, and the

Empty button determines whether or not empty methods (those containing no code) will be displayed in the list.

Creating Objects

When you highlight a class, an icon appears above the class list. For visual classes such as forms and controls, this provides an easy way of instantiating (creating objects from) the class. Just open the Form Designer in the background, click on the Class Browser, and drag the icon onto the form. Visual FoxPro creates an object from the highlighted class and adds it to the form. The icon itself can be specified inside the Class Designer.

 TIP: There is a shortcut for assigning an icon to a class. Right-click on the icon in the Class Browser, and Visual FoxPro brings up a dialog asking you to select a bitmap (.BMP) file.

If the highlighted class is a visual class, you can use a similar technique to create an object and run it. Drag the icon onto the Visual FoxPro desktop instead of onto the Form Designer, and the object is created and is executed. The Visual FoxPro desktop is actually a form, which is why this technique works. Any control can be dragged from the Class Browser to the desktop. However, because there is no way to close the desktop without quitting, the controls remain on the desktop until you exit Visual FoxPro.

Filtering the Class Hierarchy

To search for a specific class, click on the Find icon (⚏) on the Class Browser toolbar. If you're not sure of the class name, but

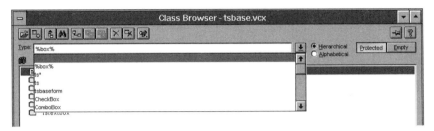

Figure 5–3. *The* **Type** *list box.*

you know what kind of class it is (for example, form or check box), enter the type in the **Type** box. The Class Browser filters the classes to include only those that match the type you specify. When you want to remove the filter, just delete the text in the **Type** box.

The **Type** box can accept standard wildcards such as ? and * in the class name. For example, to show only the classes beginning with "TS," you would enter TS* in the **Type** box. The browser also accepts the % symbol to specify characters that can appear anywhere in the class name. For example, entering %box% would filter the list to include only classes with the word "box" anywhere in the class name.

The **Type** box also keeps a history of the filters you've applied during the current browser session. These appear above the names of the built-in classes, when you pull down the Type list, as you can see in Figure 5–3.

Adding New Classes

One of the great things about the Class Browser is that you can use it as a central control point for all your class creation and manipulation. It's much easier to create classes by highlighting the superclass and clicking on a button than by writing .PRG files.

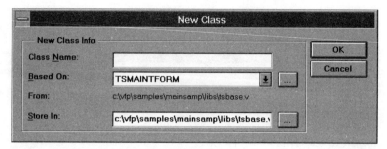

Figure 5–4. *The New Class dialog.*

To add a new class, click on the **New Class** button ( ). This displays the New Class dialog shown in Figure 5–4. In this dialog, you can specify the name of the new class, its superclass, and the visual class library in which it will be stored. By default, Visual FoxPro uses the currently highlighted class as the superclass, but you can change this if you wish.

Once you've chosen a name for your new class, the Class Designer is launched and you can add methods and properties. For more information, see the section Adding New Methods and Properties, later in this chapter.

Modifying Classes

The **Redefine Class** button ( ) allows you to move the highlighted class to a different place in the class hierarchy by changing its superclass. The Redefine Class dialog is shown in Figure 5–5.

To specify a new superclass, type its name in the **As** text box. You must type a valid class name, or the redefinition cannot take place. The **To** box specifies the name of the visual class library in which the new superclass is found. This defaults to the current class library.

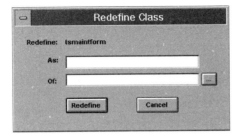

Figure 5–5. *The Redefine Class dialog.*

If you just want to rename a class but keep its hierarchical position the same, use the **Rename Class** button (⊡). *Be careful when you do this.* If you rename a class that has subclasses, the subclasses are effectively "orphaned." In other words, the subclasses inherit from a class that no longer exists. Orphan classes can only be seen when the browser is in alphabetical mode because they are no longer part of a valid hierarchy.

TIP: Avoid renaming classes that already have subclasses.

Adding New Class Libraries

You can open a new class library in the Class Browser in three ways:

1. Use the **New Library** button (📂) to open a new library in place of the current one.

2. Use the **Additional Library** button (🗎) to add the new library to those already displayed.

3. Double-click on the folder beside a class name that has a chevron.

When you add an additional class library, its classes are inserted at the appropriate places in the existing hierarchy.

TIP: Despite its name, the Class Browser can also open forms stored in .SCX files. This allows you to redefine the form's class, create code listings, change method and property descriptions, and so on.

Copying Classes

The Class Browser is created from a Visual FoxPro form, which means that you can open several browsers at once. This is the easiest way to copy a class from one class library to another: open two browsers (one for each library) and drag the class from one to the other. This is equivalent to using the ADD CLASS command.

Documenting Classes

Sometimes it's useful to see a source code listing for the classes you've created. A typical use is for application documentation: many companies require printouts of all the source code for an application.

To produce a source code listing, click on the **View Class Code** button (🔳). This produces an export file that you can print. The following code listing shows the export file for the TSMaintForm class in the SAMPLES\MAINSAMP\LIBS\TSBase.VCX library:

```
1. **************************************************
2. * Class:   tsmaintform (c:\vfp\samples\mainsamp\libs\tsbase.vcx)
3. * ParentClass:tsbaseform (c:\vfp\samples\mainsamp\libs\tsbase.vcx)
```

```
 4. * BaseClass:    form
 5. * The base form from which all maintenance style forms are based.
 6. *
 7. #INCLUDE "c:\vfp\samples\mainsamp\include\tastrade.h"
 8. *
 9. DEFINE CLASS tsmaintform AS tsbaseform
10.
11.
12.    ScaleMode = 3
13.    DoCreate = .T.
14.    Name = "tsmaintform"
15.    PROTECTED restorewindowpos
16.    PROTECTED savewindowpos
17.    PROTECTED addtomenu
18.    PROTECTED removefrommenu
19.
20.
21.    ADD OBJECT pageframe1 AS pageframe WITH ;
22.      ErasePage = .T., ;
23.      PageCount = 2, ;
24.      Top = 0, ;
25.      Left = 0, ;
26.      Width = 577, ;
27.      Height = 301, ;
28.      Name = "pageframe1", ;
29.      Page1.FontSize = 8, ;
30.      Page1.Caption = "\<Data Entry", ;
31.      Page1.Name = "Page1", ;
32.      Page2.FontSize = 8, ;
33.      Page2.Caption = "\<List", ;
34.      Page2.Name = "Page2"
35.
36.
37.    ADD OBJECT tsmaintform.pageframe1.page2.grdlist AS tsgrid WITH;
38.      Left = 0, ;
39.      ReadOnly = .T., ;
40.      RecordSource = "", ;
41.      TabIndex = 1, ;
```

```
42.     Top = 0, ;
43.     Name = "grdList"
44.
45.
46.   PROCEDURE addnew
47.     *-- (c) Microsoft Corporation 1995
48.
49.     *-- Autoselect the data entry page
50.     thisform.Pageframe1.ActivePage = 1
51.     tsBaseForm::AddNew()
52.     ENDPROC
53.
54.
55.   PROCEDURE pageframe1.Page1.Activate
56.     * Make sure form is updated whenever we switch pages. Record
57.     * pointer may have changed while another page was active.
58.     thisform.RefreshForm()
59.     ENDPROC
60.
61.
62.   PROCEDURE pageframe1.Page2.Init
63.     *-- Position the grid relative to the page
64.     this.grdList.Top = 0
65.     this.grdList.Left = 0
66.     ENDPROC
67.
68.
69.   PROCEDURE pageframe1.Page2.Activate
70.     LOCAL lcAlias
71.     lcAlias = thisform.DataEnvironment.InitialSelectedAlias
72.     IF !EMPTY(lcAlias)
73.       SELECT (lcAlias)
74.     ENDIF
75.
76.     *-- Check if any changes were made and propmt user to save
77.     *-- if necessary before changing to List page
78.     IF thisform.IsNewAndEmpty()
79.       thisform.Restore()
```

```
 80.      ELSE
 81.        IF thisform.DataChanged() AND
 82.           thisform.AskToSave() = IDCANCEL
 83.           thisform.pageframe1.ActivePage = 1
 84.          RETURN
 85.        ENDIF
 86.      ENDIF
 87.      thisform.RefreshForm()
 88.      this.grdList.SetFocus()
 89.      ENDPROC
 90.
 91.
 92.    PROCEDURE grdlist.Init
 93.      *-- Set all grid columns to read only
 94.      this.SetAll("ReadOnly", .T., "Column")
 95.      ENDPROC
 96.
 97.
 98. ENDDEFINE
 99. *
100. *-- EndDefine: tsmaintform
101. ****************************************************
```

As you'll notice if you pull down the File menu while this export window is visible, all you can do with this listing is print it. It was intended as a way for you to print source code listings as documentation for a class library or application. You can copy the listing to the clipboard and paste it into a .PRG file, but it may not work, especially if it uses code that is specific to class definitions contained in .VCX files.

Customizing the Class Browser

Because the Class Browser is created from a Visual FoxPro form, it can be customized. Obviously, before you can modify the properties of the browser, you have to have a browser object. To do this, choose the **Class Browser** option from the

Tools menu in order to create the public system variable
_OBROWSER.

You can use the following syntax to access class browser properties:

`_OBROWSER.Caption = "Savannah's Browser"`

To open the Class Browser you've just created, use the DO command as follows:

`DO (_BROWSER)`

The Class Browser is actually provided as an application whose filename is Browser.APP. If you decide to use your own browser instead of the one provided by Microsoft, simply use the configuration file to assign its name to the _BROWSER system variable. For example,

`_BROWSER = "MyBrowser.APP"`

 TIP: The _BROWSER system variable is not the same as the _OBROWSER system variable. The first contains the name of the browser application being used, whereas the second refers to the current browser object.

Specifying Add-In Programs

One of the ways in which you can extend the functionality of the Class Browser is by specifying add-in programs. These are program (.PRG), form (.SCX), application (.APP), executable (.EXE), or compiled program (.FXP) files that are run when a particular Class Browser method is called by an event.

For example, to run MyProgram.PRG whenever a request is made to add a new class, use the following syntax:

```
_OBROWSER.AddIn( "Run My Program", "MyProgram.PRG", "NewClass")
```

The first parameter represents the name of the options that will be added to the Class Browser's Add-In menu. The second parameter is the program to be executed when that option is selected. The third parameter is the name of the Class Browser method that will cause the add-in program to be run automatically.

 TIP: Look at the documentation topic for "Class Browser Methods" to see a complete list of methods that can be used with Class Browser objects.

The Class Designer

The Class Designer is invoked in one of three ways:

1. Double-click on a class in the Class Browser.

2. Create a new class via the File menu.

3. Issue the CREATE CLASS or MODIFY CLASS commands.

The Class Designer can be used to create both visual and nonvisual classes. It allows you to use menu options to add methods and properties to a class, instead of having to write class definitions using DEFINE CLASS statements. The Class Designer looks very similar to the Form Designer, as you can see from Figure 5–6.

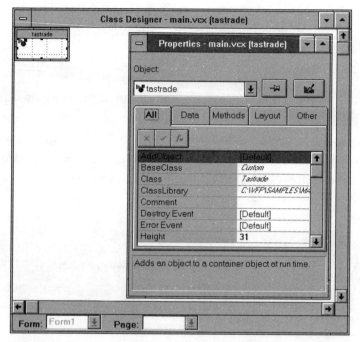

Figure 5–6. *The Class Designer, showing the TasTrade class.*

In fact, in this example we're editing the TasTrade nonvisual class in the Main.VCX library provided with the Tasmanian Traders sample application. Because it's a nonvisual class, nothing but an icon is displayed. For container classes, the Form Controls toolbar is available, and the screen looks very much like the Form Designer. The important difference is that because we're editing a class, any changes we make will affect all containers (including forms) that were created from that class.

Adding New Methods and Properties

To add a new method or property, use the **New Method** and **New Property** options on the Class menu. These options both use basically the same dialog, shown in Figure 5–7.

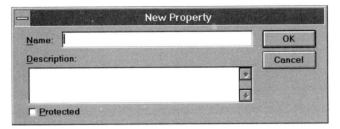

Figure 5–7. *The New Property/New Method dialog.*

It's important to add a description in this dialog because this is the description that appears in the description box at the bottom right corner of the Class Browser when you highlight the method or property. In fact, this is one of the reasons to use the Class Designer instead of writing classes manually.

When you add a new property, its value defaults to False (.F.). To change this value, select it in the Properties window just as you would any other property. When you add a new method, you're actually adding only its name; you must still double-click on the method in the Properties window to add code.

In the Properties window, properties and methods inherited from Visual FoxPro classes are shown in propercase (first letter capitalized). The properties and methods you've added appear in lowercase at the end of the list, as shown in Figure 5–8.

Modifying Methods and Properties

To modify a property or method that you've added via the Class menu, use the **Edit Property/Method** option on the Class menu. This displays the dialog shown in Figure 5–9.

The list box shows only the properties and methods that you've added, not those that you inherited from the original Visual

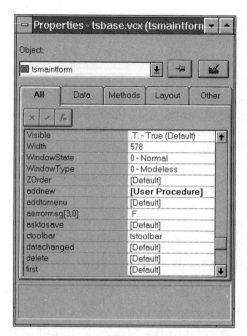

Figure 5–8. *The Properties window for TSMaintForm.*

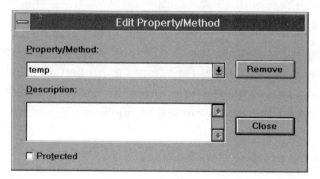

Figure 5–9. *The Edit Property/Method dialog.*

FoxPro base class. You can use this dialog to modify the description or scope, or to remove the property or method entirely.

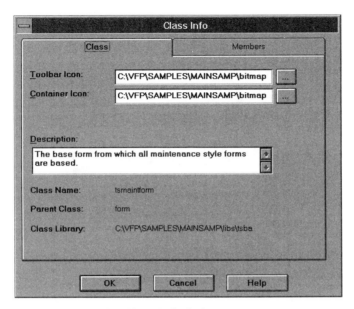

Figure 5–10. *The Class Info dialog.*

Adding Class Information

The **Class Info** option on the Class menu brings up the dialog shown in Figure 5–10. As with properties and methods, the description is important because it appears in the bottom left section of the Class Browser.

Two icons that can be assigned to a class:

1. The Toolbar icon is used when you choose to add your own classes to the Form Controls toolbar.

2. The Container icon is the icon that you use in the Class Browser to drag objects onto forms.

The second page of the Class Info dialog (shown in Figure 5–11) shows all the properties and methods for this class, and allows you to easily apply the Protected scope. For object members

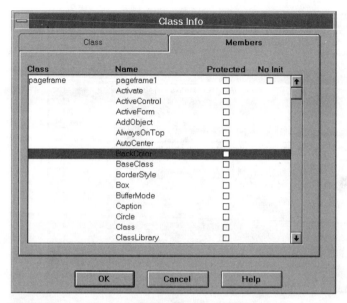

Figure 5-11. *Page 2 of the Class Info dialog.*

(properties that are objects of other classes), you can also click on a check box to add the NOINIT clause to the ADD OBJECT statement that's used in the class's constructor.

The fact that the object members in this dialog allow you to check a NOINIT clause tells you that they're being added to the class with the ADD OBJECT command. To verify this, use the **View Class Code** button in the Class Browser to see a source code listing. Remember to watch for cyclical constructor calls if the object members are themselves containers.

Specifying an Include File

An *include file* (also known as a *header file*, hence the .H extension) is a file that contains constants representing common values. For example, the company name to display in window titles might be represented by a constant called

COMPANY_NAME. You can use this constant in your programs, and Visual FoxPro will replace it at compile time with whatever value it contains. The advantage is that your code is easier to read, and you can easily change the value of the constant without having to change every piece of code in which it is used.

To add or modify the include file for the class currently being edited, choose the **Include File** option on the Class menu and select the desired file. This is equivalent to typing #include <fileName> at the top of a .PRG file containing a hand-coded class definition.

Include files can be found in the **Text Files** section of the **Other** tab on the Project Manager. The following include file, TasTrade.H, is included with the TasTrade sample application:

```
 1. *-- (c) Microsoft Corporation 1995
 2.
 3. *-- Common include file
 4. #INCLUDE "FOXPRO.H"
 5. #INCLUDE "STRINGS.H"
 6.
 7. #DEFINE DEBUGMODE   .F.
 8. #DEFINE INIFILE     "TASTRADE.INI"
 9. #DEFINE CRLF        CHR(13) + CHR(10)
10. #DEFINE CR          CHR(13)
11. #DEFINE TAB         CHR(9)
12.
13. #DEFINE CURRENCY      "$"
14. #DEFINE AERRORARRAY  7
15.
16. *-- These constants are used in tsbaseform to
17. *-- indicate the status of the current alias
18. #DEFINE FILE_OK      0
19. #DEFINE FILE_BOF     1
20. #DEFINE FILE_EOF     2
21. #DEFINE FILE_CANCEL  3
```

```
22.
23. *-- Constants to identify which trigger failed
24. *-- using element 5 of the array returned by
25. *-- AERROR(), as well as to reference the appropriate
26. *-- array element in the error message array: aErrorMsg[]
27. #DEFINE INSERTTRIG   1
28. #DEFINE UPDATETRIG   2
29. #DEFINE DELETETRIG   3
30.
31. *-- Constants used to read the system registry
32. #DEFINE HKEY_LOCAL_MACHINE        -2147483646
33. #DEFINE KEY_SHARED_TOOLS_LOCATION  ;
34.    "Software\Microsoft\Shared Tools Location"
35. #DEFINE KEY_NTCURRENTVERSION        ;
36.    "Software\Microsoft\Windows NT\CurrentVersion"
37. #DEFINE KEY_WIN4CURRENTVERSION     ;
38.    "Software\Microsoft\Windows\CurrentVersion"
39. #DEFINE KEY_QUERY_VALUE            1
40. #DEFINE ERROR_SUCCESS              0
```

When to Use the Visual Tools

Visual FoxPro provides us with three ways of creating classes:

1. The Class Designer

2. The Form Designer with the **Save As Class** option on the File menu

3. Hand-coded program files

Most of the classes you create can best be created in the Class Designer. The Form Designer is a useful tool, but it doesn't provide the Class Info menu that's available in the Class Designer.

It is possible even to create visual classes using the Program Editor. However, this seems unnecessarily masochistic! It's much easier to use the Class Designer with the Form Controls toolbar visible.

 TIP: Some classes, such as the DataEnvironment base class, cannot be subclassed visually. In these cases, you'll have to use the Program Editor.

Summary

As you can see, Visual FoxPro's tools are pretty powerful, and they allow you to perform most tasks related to class development. And because the Class Browser was written in Visual FoxPro, it can be customized and extended at will. In Chapter 6, we'll look at a perennial problem facing designers of object-oriented code: translating objects into relational databases.

6

Databases

One of the most common questions when working with object technology is: How do I communicate with a database? Because most of us are working with .DBF files, we obviously can't store an object directly into the database without first performing some kind of translation. Or can we? Some of you may have heard of object databases—databases in which objects can be stored in something close to their native format. Although this technology is still being developed, it's worth taking the time to understand the concepts behind object databases.

This chapter looks at two ways of handling databases in object-oriented systems. First, I'll explain how to deconstruct an object into a .DBF file using Visual FoxPro's DataEnvironment class. Then I'll present some of the theory behind the way in which an object database works.

Working with .DBF Files

In an object-oriented system, classes can be thought of as data types. However, because the .DBF file format only supports character, numeric, data, logical, and memo data types, we obviously can't store our system objects directly in the database. Instead, we must first translate them into a form that the database can understand.

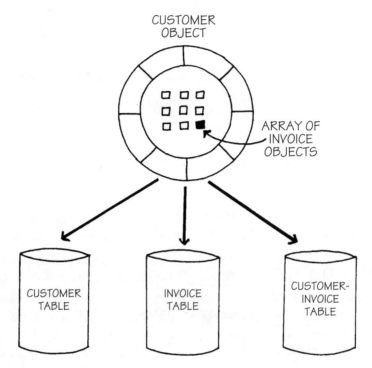

Figure 6–1. *Breaking objects down into relational tables.*

Another problem is that our objects model real-life things, whereas a relational database structure does not. As seen in Figure 6–1, our system may have a customer object that contains invoice objects for all the products that that customer has ordered. However, our database structure typically has separate customer and invoice tables, related on a common key field.

It's tempting to avoid the whole issue by modeling the system classes on the database structures, and that may be a valid technique for certain systems. However, it's generally more flexible to create classes that model the business in the real world, rather than tying your design to a particular database structure. What happens if the data structure changes?

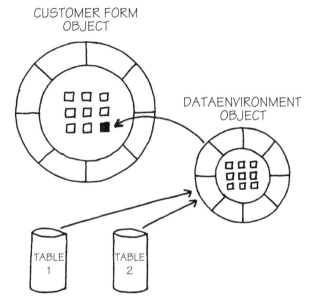

Figure 6–2. *The DataEnvironment class.*

Another advantage to this technique is the ease with which you can later switch to another database engine. You don't have to change your system classes at all—just the data sources.

The DataEnvironment Class

Visual FoxPro makes the process of storing data in a table much easier with the DataEnvironment class. (See Figure 6–2.) Every form that you create can have a Data Environment object inside it. This DataEnvironment object contains cursor and relation objects for the current form. In other words, the data environment stores a set of tables that can be used by the form and shows the relationships between those tables.

Table 6–1 shows the properties, methods, and events in the DataEnvironment class.

Table 6–1. *The Properties, Methods, and Events in the*
DataEnvironment Class

Member Name	Description
Properties	
AutoOpenTables	Specifies whether the object's tables and views are automatically opened when the form, formSet or report is opened.
AutoCloseTables	Specifies whether the object's tables and views are closed when the form, formSet or report is released.
InitialSelectedAlias	The alias selected when the object is loaded.
Name	The object's name.
Methods	
AddObject	Adds an object to the container at runtime.
RemoveObject	Removes an object from the container at runtime.
CloseTables	Closes the object's tables and views.
OpenTables	Opens the object's tables and views.
Events	
AFterCloseTables	Occurs after the object's tables and views are closed.
BeforeOpenTables	Occurs before the object's tables and views are opened.
Destroy	Occurs when the object is released.
Error	Occurs when there's a runtime error in one of the object's methods.
Init	Occurs when the object is created.

To see the data environment for a form, right-click on the form in the Form Designer and choose the **Data Environment** option from the shortcut menu. This launches the Data Environment Designer, which is shown in Figure 6–3.

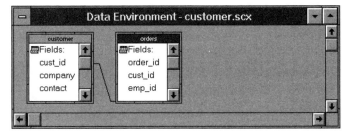

Figure 6–3. *The Data Environment Designer.*

TIP: The DataEnvironment class cannot be sub-classed visually. To subclass, you must hand-code the changes using the Program Editor.

The tables that you add to the data environment will appear in the ControlSource property for any data-bound controls on the form. In this way, Visual FoxPro allows you to tie controls directly to tables, without having to scatter and gather to intermediate memory variables or properties.

To add tables or views to the Data Environment Designer, you can either drag them from the Project Manager or choose the **Add Table** option from the Data Environment menu.

You may notice that some tables or views have a line drawn between them like the one shown in Figure 6–3. This represents a relation and will be drawn automatically if the designer sees that a persistent relation has been created for these two tables or views in the Database Designer. You can also create temporary relations between tables or views just for this

DataEnvironment object. Simply drag a field from one table onto an index on the same field name in the other table.

 TIP: The Data Environment Designer is only available from inside the Form Designer, not from the Class Designer.

Data-Bound Controls

Like many Windows language, Visual FoxPro supports what are known as *data-bound controls*. These controls are directly linked to fields in tables or views, and they remove the need to use memory variables as intermediate data buffers.

To bind a control to a data source, just select the control, go to the Properties window, and set the `ControlSource` or `RecordSource` property to the appropriate field. When a DataEnvironment object has been added to the form you're working with, these properties will actually be list boxes that contain the fields from all the tables and views in the DataEnvironment object. This is a convenient way to bind controls to the data in the DataEnvironment object, and removes the need to hand-code table and view names.

Downsides of Data-Bound Controls

Although the data-bound controls are very easy to use, they do tie your class designs to a specific language. For example, if I were to create a class that stored DbfTable objects as properties and had its own `Load`, `Edit`, and `Save` methods, I could implement the design in any language. However, by building that functionality into the controls on a form, I'm making it difficult to implement in, say, Smalltalk. This trade-off is one you should consider carefully. For most developers, the downside is acceptable when compared to the power and ease of use of data-bound controls.

DBFTable Classes

If Visual FoxPro had not provided the DataEnvironment class, the process of dismantling an object into a database table would be much more complicated. We'd have to create a DbfTable class and put an object of that class into each of our business classes. That's a much more language-independent way of working with databases, but it requires a lot more effort from individual developers.

Object Databases

Up until now we have dealt only with .DBF databases. Unfortunately, the .DBF file format has a number of shortcomings, including the inability to store objects as native object files. This section focuses on a possible solution to .DBF inefficiencies: the use of object databases.

Why Use an Object Database?

While object database technology is still relatively new compared to relational databases, it is becoming accepted by more and more companies with an investment in object orientation. Here are the most common reasons that people investigate object databases:

- A desire to store complete objects rather than breaking them down using the techniques just described.

- A need to achieve better performance for complex data types like objects.

- A need to maintain information about the state of the application from execution to execution, and to be able to reload the application in exactly the same state it was in when it was last exited.

- A need to store classes for use in multiprogrammer environments.

The following sections look at the requirements in more detail.

Storing Complex Data Types

Traditional database management systems (DBMSs) can only store certain types of data, typically things like character, numeric, date, logical, and so on. However, we've already established that object-oriented systems deal with much more complex data types. In addition, one of the major benefits of object orientation is that it allows you to define your own data types. Obviously it's not practical to wait for the DBMS vendors to change their products to support your own data types.

Some people suggest using Binary Large Objects (BLOBs) to store object data. Although this may work for simple objects, BLOBs have several limitations, including the inability to nest BLOBs within other BLOBs. This makes it impossible to store container objects without first breaking them down, at which point we may as well be using .DBF files.

Improving Performance

An object database is one that's designed to store objects in their entirety, without having to break them down to fit a relational model. But what about speed? After all, that was one of our reasons for using an object database in the first place. Well, most people find that a traditional DBMS is faster than an object database (OODBMS) for simple transactions, but that an object database performs much faster for more complex data types. That makes sense because an object database doesn't have the overhead of having to search for data across multiple tables.

Here's an example of the increased efficiency of an object database.[1] The U.S. Navy was developing a materials acquisition system that stored parts information in a graphical way. They found the relational database to be extremely slow at manipulating the complex data types that the system required. For example, it took 15 minutes to store the geometry necessary to display a printed circuit board consisting of 2500 components.

The Navy loaded the same data into an object database and ran a comparison test. The same data storage took only 9 seconds. That's a speed improvement of two orders of magnitude! They found similar improvements with data retrieval. Now, I'm not suggesting that this level of improvement will be found in every case, but it's possible when dealing with complex data.

Another benefit of using an object database is the improved referential integrity that comes from storing all the data together rather than spreading it out across several tables. Obviously the fewer tables involved, the less chance that they will get out of sync.

Persistent Object Stores

Our third reason for investigating object databases was a need to maintain information about the state of the application from

---

1. From David Taylor's *Object-Oriented Information Systems: Planning and Implementation* (see Appendix B).

execution to execution, and to be able to reload the application in exactly the same state it was in when it was last exited. Obviously this is much easier if all the components of the application—its windows, menus, reports, and so on—are objects that keep track of their current contents and coordinates. Products like Smalltalk do this automatically by saving an image of the system every time you exit. The next time the system is entered, the previous image is reloaded. The result is that you have the same windows on the screen, the same tables open, and even the same memory variables loaded.

The Smalltalk method works fine in a single-user system, but it fails in a multiuser environment. It makes no attempt to handle security, locking, referential integrity, or any of the other concerns that arise in a networked application.

With relational databases, the only solution to the multiuser image problem is to translate the system into records in tables, which has exactly the same drawbacks that we mentioned previously. Even though we're now dealing with a series of environment states rather than traditional data, an object database is still a logical choice.

Component Repositories

Our final reason for moving to an object database was a need to store classes for use in multiprogrammer environments. Object orientation is supposed to help you reuse code, but that's no good unless you have a way of accessing that code.

Some people try to adapt existing source code version-control systems to use as component repositories. This is a partial solution, but we really need more than just control over the source code.

We also need concurrency controls, the ability to check classes in and out, and so on. These are typical functions of a database.

Because we're storing complex data—in this case, source code and documentation for classes—an object database is once again a good choice. Not only that, but because we're already storing objects, it makes sense to use the same database engine to store the class definitions.

Currently it's difficult to find a language-independent component repository (that's the name for an object database that's designed to store classes or prebuilt software components). Most repositories support C++ and some support Smalltalk, but most require that all the components you store be written in the same language. There are a couple of exceptions. Servio's Gem-Stone stores everything in its own Opal format, but it allows you to translate classes to and from Smalltalk and C++. The VERSANT system stores C++ and Smalltalk components in close-to-native format, but it only permits them to be accessed from the original language or from C.

Future Features

Although the browsers and inspectors found in many object-oriented languages are a significant enhancement over the tools we have available in procedural languages, they are still not sufficient for use with a large-scale component repository. Traditional browsers are simply too slow when used with thousands of classes.

We need a browser that is attached to the repository and can scan what's inside. In an ideal world, a programmer could list a set of responsibilities for a class and ask the repository to return a list of the nearest matches. Currently the Object Management

Group (OMG) is working on a version of structured query language (SQL) for object databases. Once that becomes a reality, it should be a relatively simple matter to use standard SQL commands to fill a class browser.

The Structure of an Object Database

So far, we've talked about all the things an object database can do. But how does it do them, exactly?

An object database usually consists of three basic components: an *object manager*, an *object server*, and an *object store*. Your application talks to the object manager, which uses the object server to gain access to the object store.

Most object databases allow you to combine the object managers and servers in different ways. For example, you could have several different applications, each using its own object manager and server to access a common object store. Alternatively, you could have an application that accesses multiple object stores, using a separate manager and server for each store (actually this is a limited form of distributed object management).

Of the three components, the object store is the easiest to understand. It's simply a physical storage system that resides on a hard disk. The other two components are a little more complex and warrant further explanation.

Object Manager

The object manager manages a local cache of objects for an individual application (Figure 6–4). Each application uses its object manager to check out objects from the object store and then check them back in again when they have finished using them.

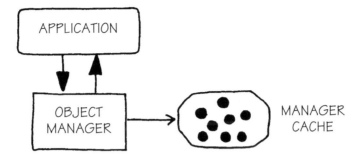

Figure 6–4. *The role of the object manager.*

New objects and modifications to existing objects are carried out in the local cache first. When the transactions have been completed, the resulting objects are committed to the object store. This process, together with tasks like managing the login and logout processes, are performed by the object manager working in conjunction with the object server.

The object manager is also responsible for performing any necessary translation between the program object formats and the database object formats. For example, the GemStone object manager converts program objects from C++ to Opal and back again.

Object Server

The object server is responsible for managing another, separate cache of objects that is shared by many applications. It uses a series of locking mechanisms to coordinate the requests from different applications to access the object store. The role of the object server is shown in Figure 6–5. It's important to note that, unlike the object manager, the cache used by the object server is shared by many applications.

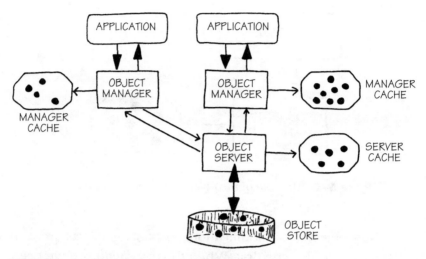

Figure 6-5. *The role of the object server.*

The object server is also responsible for handling the different physical formats on the machines with which it's working. For example, if the object manager is running on a Sun machine and the object server is running on an IBM RS/6000, the object server will translate the data storage formats so that the Sun can access the object store correctly.

Leading Object Databases

Object databases haven't been in existence for as long as relational databases, but they're no longer "bleeding edge" technology. Table 6-2 lists some of the leading object databases together with their major customers.

Table 6–2. *Leading Object Databases*

Product/ Company	Platforms	Languages	First Released	Key Customers
Gemstone Gemstone Systems Beaverton, OR (503) 629-8383	Windows, Windows NT, Mac, OS/ 2, UNIX	C, C++, Smalltalk	1987	Florida Power & Light, J. P. Morgan, Texas Instruments
Illustra Server Ilustra Information Technologies Oakland, CA (510) 652-8000	Windows NT, UNIX	C, C++, Visual Basic, SQL, ODBC	1993	America Online, Sun Microsystems
Matisse ADB Redwood Shores, CA (415) 610-0367	Windows, Windows NT, Mac, UNIX, VMS	C, C++	1992	Tokyo Gas, US Navy, France Telecom
Objectivity/DB Objectivity Mountain View, CA (415) 254-7100	Windows, Windows NT, UNIX, VMS	C, C++, Smalltalk, SQL, ODBC	1990	Citibank, Motorola, British Telecom
ObjectStore Object Design Burlington, MA (617) 674-5000	Windows, Windows NT, OS/2, UNIX, VMS	C, C++, Smalltalk	1990	New York Stock Exchange, MCI, Ford
ODB-II Fujitsu Open Systems Solutions San Jose, CA (408) 432-1300 (800) 545-6774	UNIX	C, C++	1994	Mazda, Australian Bureau of Statistics, Yamanouchi Pharmaceutical
Ontos DB Ontos Burlington, MA (617) 272-7110	UNIX, Windows NT in 1995	C++, SQL	1989	R.R. Donnelley, British Telecom, AT&T

Table 6–2. *Leading Object Databases (continued)*

Product/ Company	Platforms	Languages	First Released	Key Customers
O2 System O2 Technology Mountai View, CA (415) 969-2333	Windows, Windows NT, Mac, UNIX	C, C++, SQL, ODBC	1990	AT&T, Electricite de France, Aerospatiale
Poet Poet Software San Mateo, CA (415) 286-4640	Windows, Windows NT, Mac, OS/ 2, UNIX	C++, SQL, ODBC	1991	Associated Press, CompuServe, EDS
UniSQL Server UniSQL Austin, TX (512) 343-7297 (800) 451-3267	Windows, Windows NT, UNIX	C, C++, Smalltalk, SQL, ODBC	1992	Westinghouse, Mobil Oil, US Air Force
Versant ODBMS Versant Menlo Park, CA (415) 329-7500	Windows NT, OS/2, UNIX	C, C++, Smalltalk	1990	Ameritech, Scotia Bank, Business Systems Corp. of America

Table reprinted from *Information Week*, July 17, 1995

Summary

Currently Visual FoxPro developers are faced with the problem of deconstructing objects into relational databases. Because most object databases provide only C++ or Smalltalk classes, they cannot be used with Visual FoxPro applications. However, it's up to us as developers to let object database vendors know that there's a market here waiting to be serviced. We need to make it clear that Visual FoxPro is now an object-oriented language, and we'd like vendors to provide Visual FoxPro versions of their object database classes. If the demand is there, you can bet that most vendors will try to meet it.

Now that you understand how to create classes in Visual Fox-Pro and what the problems of data storage are, let's look at the somewhat unique approach to designing applications using an object-oriented language.

7

Analysis and Design

You now understand the meanings of terms such as *object*, *class*, *method*, and so forth. But that still doesn't tell you how to write object-oriented applications. It's one thing to know what a class is, but it's quite another to know how best to design one. This chapter concentrates on how to decide what classes you need and what they should do; in short, how to design object-oriented applications.

The Software Life Cycle

The software life cycle is the name given to the process of designing, implementing, and testing a system. It traditionally starts with a requirements specification, although the scope of this document still varies widely from person to person. The specification spawns the system design, which is eventually implemented as a system. This section compares the life cycle of an object-oriented system with the more traditional waterfall model.

The Traditional Life Cycle

The traditional software life cycle is known as the *waterfall model* because it is presented as a series of cascading steps. The development process is split into stages, with each stage starting as the preceding one finishes. The usual stages are analysis, design, coding, testing, and maintenance; these stages are shown in Figure 7–1.

The waterfall model has several problems:

1. It doesn't provide sufficient flexibility to incorporate user feedback. For example, the results of the testing phase may force portions of the system to reenter the design phase.

2. It rarely produces systems that meet user requirements. Users often don't know exactly what they want until they see a prototype, at which point it's hard to make design changes without going back to the beginning of the entire process.

3. Although it may look good on paper, the waterfall model is rarely followed "to the letter" in a development process. Instead, companies skip from

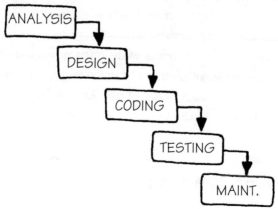

Figure 7–1. *The waterfall model.*

section to section, often with little control or organization to the process.

4. It takes too long. Applications that are developed using the waterfall model typically take months or years to develop and are often obsolete by the time they are delivered.

The Object-Oriented Life Cycle

Just as object-oriented systems are said to more accurately model the real world, so the object-oriented life cycle more accurately reflects the real-world design process. (See Figure 7–2.) Instead of a series of stages that must each be completed before the next stage can be entered, the life cycle is a series of steps that are completed and reentered as necessary. And the evolution and modification of the system is built into the model, rather than being ignored.

This model is similar to the waterfall model, except that modification is built in. You may continue to follow the waterfall model for individual classes or groups of classes.

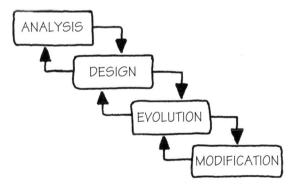

Figure 7–2. *The object-oriented life cycle.*

In an object-oriented system, the real-life entities that are discussed in the requirements specification actually become objects in the design phase and continue to become software objects during coding.

One of the key differences between the traditional and object-oriented life cycles is the amount of time spent in the design phase. It has been estimated that as much as 70 percent of the development cycle is spent on analysis and design. Because the classes we design will be reused in many other applications, it's important that the design is correct from the beginning. In fact, this is one of the major benefits of object technology—we're developing classes that model the real world and can be used in many different ways, rather than just writing a piece of software to solve one particular problem.

One major difficulty faced by many companies moving to object-oriented technology is that of corporate reorganization. Many corporations are organized much like the traditional waterfall method, with departments of designers, programmers, testers, users, and so on. Although it isn't necessary to completely redesign the organization chart, it is essential that a vehicle be in place to facilitate the communication between these different departments. Ideally, work teams should be organized by project rather than by department and should consist of class designers, coders, and testers. This concept is explained further in Chapter 8.

Nouns versus Verbs

It has often been said that procedural programming concentrates on the verbs in a problem, whereas object orientation focuses on the nouns. Let's look at an example from *Object-Oriented Software* by Winblad, Edwards, and King (see Appendix B). The following paragraph describes the functionality of a word processing system, with the key words underlined.

The word processing system allows <u>creation</u> of documents. Created documents are <u>saved</u> on a user's directory. Users can <u>print</u> or <u>display</u> documents. Documents can be <u>changed</u>. Documents can be <u>deleted</u> from a user's directory.

This is how we would look at the system if we were designing it procedurally. The preceding paragraph tells us that we need Create, Save, Print, Display, Change, and Delete routines. Compare this to the same paragraph with the focus altered to reflect an object-oriented design:

The <u>word processing system</u> allows creation of <u>documents</u>. Created <u>documents</u> are saved on a <u>user</u>'s <u>directory</u>. Users can print or display <u>documents</u>. <u>Documents</u> can be changed. <u>Documents</u> can be deleted from a <u>user</u>'s <u>directory</u>.

This paragraph is telling us that our system needs to handle Documents, Directories, and Users. These will probably become classes in our application. The portions of the paragraph that are not underlined further inform us that certain classes must be able to create, save, print, display, change, and delete.

The Basic Design Steps

When designing an object-oriented application, we generally take four basic steps. These are:

1. Finding the entities
2. Defining the responsibilities

3. Defining the attributes

4. Finding the relationships

This section looks at each of these steps in more detail.

Finding the Entities

The first step in designing an object-oriented application is to define the entities involved. Sit down and list all the possible entities. For example, in my insurance application, it was immediately obvious that I needed to handle policies and insurers, and a little more probing revealed that I also had to be aware of coverages, reinsurers, accounts, and checks. Try not to think of these as objects or classes, but rather as "things" with which your system must interact.

You'll probably end up with a long list that includes things like employees, customers, and other noncomputer entities. Try not to focus on databases at this point—just on the business entities involved. Now it's time to move on to the next step.

Defining the Responsibilities

For each entity on your list, write down the things that the entity must be responsible for doing. For example, a "check" entity must print and post itself to a ledger. A "customer" entity must request a policy, notify of claims, and so on. Make sure each responsibility is unique and well defined because these will eventually become methods in our classes. Don't worry if you can't come up with something for every entity.

Defining the Attributes

Write down a list of all the information that you think relates to each entity. It doesn't matter if there's some overlap. For example, both customers and employees will need name, address, phone number, and so on. These attributes will become properties when we implement the class.

Finding the Relationships

Now we get to the fun part! Look at the lists of responsibilities and attributes. Take the entities whose attributes significantly overlap those of another entity (for example, Customer and Employee) and put the overlapping attributes on a separate list with a generic name that describes both entities (such as Person). Now look at the responsibilities. Are there some overlaps there, too? If so, add those to the generic list. Now we're on our way to defining the relationships between our entities.

Abstraction

Remember that object orientation is all about programming the exceptions to the rule. In the preceding paragraph, we've defined a generic Person class. That class may incorporate all the necessary responsibilities for a person in your system. Alternatively it may act as an *abstract class* (a class with no instances, whose purpose is to group other, related subclasses), listing all the general information about a person, and leaving it up to the subclasses, Employee and Customer, to provide the specifics about that type of person.

You may find that some of the entities in your original list have no responsibilities or attributes. Often this means that they are not suited to becoming classes; however, you may want to keep them around for now in case they're good candidates for becoming abstract classes.

One of the goals when looking for classes is to find as many abstract classes as possible. If a responsibility or attribute is shared by several subclasses, you should design a superclass to capture the behavior in one place. This process is known as *abstraction,* or *generalization*—taking the general features of an entity and moving them to a superclass. The reverse process is *specialization,* which means moving the specifics to subclasses.

The "Is-Kind-Of" Relationship

In the previous section, we identified two classes, Employee and Customer, that are subclasses of a more generic class called Person. We could also say that an Employee *is a kind of* Person, which implies that inheritance is being used. (See Figure 7–3.)

When you're trying to figure out which classes should inherit from which superclasses, ask yourself if your proposed subclass

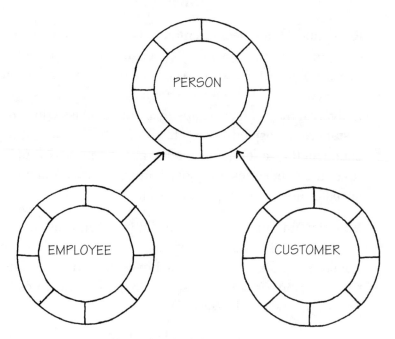

Figure 7–3. *The "is-kind-of" relationship.*

is a "kind of" superclass. For example, is a line item a kind of invoice? Obviously not. This means that the LineItem class does not inherit from the Invoice class.

The "Is-Part-Of" Relationship

The "is-part-of" relationship implies containership. (See Figure 7–4.) It can be seen in examples such as invoices, where an invoice consists of many line items. Because a line item is not a kind of invoice, the LineItem class would not inherit from the Invoice class. However, the Invoice class does have a relationship with the LineItem class because it has LineItem objects inside it.

In this example, we say that the LineItem class *is part of* the Invoice class. An object created from the Invoice class is called a composite or container object because it is made up of more than one object.

The "Has" Relationship

The "has" relationship is similar to the "is-part-of" relationship, except that the container class and its members can exist outside

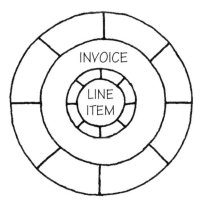

Figure 7–4. *The "is-part-of" relationship.*

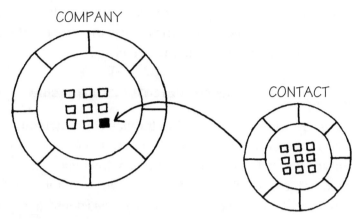

Figure 7–5. *The "Has" relationship.*

of one another. (See Figure 7–5.) For example, the Company class we looked at earlier *has* Contact objects inside it. However, it would be valid to create Contact objects without having a Company object. This is not true of an Invoice class that contains LineItem objects; the LineItem objects serve no purpose on their own.

The "Using" Relationship

"Using" relationships are commonly found at implementation time. This relationship refers to cases where a method in one class needs to *use* an object of another class, without having an object of that class as one of its properties. For example, the Print method in an Invoice class might create a Printer object, store it in a memory variable, use it, and throw it away. (See Figure 7–6.)

The "Is-Analogous-To" Relationship

When two classes look analogous (their attributes and responsibilities are similar, but not identical), it is possible that they

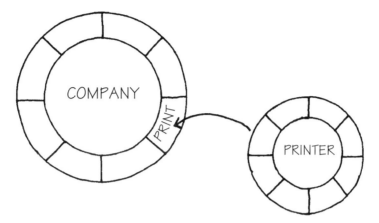

Figure 7–6. *The "Using" relationship.*

share a common superclass. Noticing analogous relationships between classes can often point out a necessary class that is missing from the class hierarchy.

CRC Cards

Many people use index cards to aid in the design process. These are known as CRC *(Class-Responsibility-Collaboration) cards.* The idea is to write on each card the name of an entity, its responsibilities (Print, Post to Ledger, and so on.) and, later on, other classes with which it may collaborate. (Collaboration means "working with" and usually implies a "using," "has," or "is-part-of" relationship.) I also find it helpful to list each entity's attributes on the back of the card. (See Figures 7–7 and 7–8.) Listing this information on a small card allows you to easily compare one entity with others and to decide where each belongs in the class hierarchy.

Class: Customer	
Responsibilities:	Collaborators:
Request policy	Insurance Policy
Notify of claims	

Figure 7–7. *CRC card (front).*

Class: Customer	
Attributes:	
Name	Age
Address	Sex
Phone	Marital status
Fax	Years insured
Company	Type of ins.

Figure 7–8. *CRC card (back).*

Where Next?

Before beginning the process of creating CRC cards and class diagrams, it's a good idea to create *use cases*—common business scenarios that the system must incorporate. Before formalizing your class design, go through each of these scenarios and make sure that your classes will allow each of them to be fulfilled.

Once you have a pretty solid idea of your classes and the relationships between them, you can use a computer-based design tool to create formal class diagrams. Some of the design tools you could use are as follows:

- ***Graphical Designer**–*Advanced Software Technologies, Inc., (800) 811-2784.

- ***System Architect**–*Popkin Software & Systems, Inc., (800) 732-5227.

- ***ICONIX PowerTools**–*ICONIX Software Engineering, Inc., (310) 458-0092.

- ***With Class**–*MicroGOLD Software, Inc., (908) 722-6438.

- ***Rational Rose**–*Rational Software Corporation, (408) 496-3600.

- ***Visio**–*Shapeware Corporation, (303) 743-9533.

The ATM Example

Let's look at a more detailed example: an ATM (Automated Teller Machine).[1] Let's assume that we need to create a set of classes that model the way an ATM works, possibly as part of a larger banking system. The following section shows the requirements specification, with the nouns underlined.

ATM Requirements Specification

An <u>automated teller machine</u> (<u>ATM</u>) is a <u>machine</u> through which <u>bank customers</u> can perform a number of the most common <u>financial transactions</u>. The <u>machine</u> consists of a <u>display screen</u>, a <u>bank card reader</u>, <u>numeric</u> and <u>special input keys</u>, a <u>money dispenser slot</u>, a <u>deposit slot</u>, and a <u>receipt printer</u>. These <u>elements</u> are arranged as shown in Figure 7–9.

---

1. This example is taken from Wirfs-Brock, Wilkerson, and Wiener's *Designing Object-Oriented Software* (see Appendix B).

When the <u>machine</u> is idle, a <u>greeting message</u> is displayed. The <u>keys</u> and <u>deposit slot</u> remain inactive until a <u>bank card</u> has been entered. When a <u>bank card</u> is inserted, the <u>card reader</u> attempts to read it. If the <u>card</u> cannot be read, the <u>user</u> is informed that the <u>card</u> is unreadable, and the <u>card</u> is ejected.

If the <u>card</u> is readable, the <u>user</u> is asked to enter a <u>personal identification number</u> (<u>PIN</u>). The <u>user</u> is given <u>feedback</u> as to the number of <u>digits</u> entered at the <u>numeric keypad</u>, but not the specific <u>digits</u> entered. If the <u>PIN</u> is entered correctly, the <u>user</u> is shown the <u>main menu</u>. Otherwise, the <u>user</u> is given up to two additional <u>chances</u> to enter the <u>PIN</u> correctly. <u>Failure</u> to do so on the <u>third try</u> causes the <u>machine</u> to keep the <u>bank card</u>. The <u>user</u> can retrieve the <u>card</u> only by dealing directly with an <u>authorized bank employee</u>.

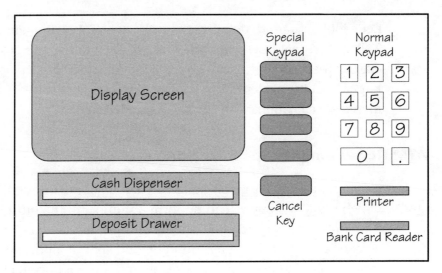

Figure 7–9. *An ATM machine.*

The <u>main menu</u> contains a <u>list of transactions</u> that can be performed. These <u>transactions</u> are:

- Deposit <u>funds</u> to an <u>account.</u>

- Withdraw <u>funds</u> from an <u>account.</u>

- Transfer <u>funds</u> from one <u>account</u> to another.

- Query the <u>balance</u> of any <u>account.</u>

The <u>user</u> can select a <u>transaction</u> and specify all relevant <u>information</u>. When a <u>transaction</u> has been completed, the <u>system</u> returns to the <u>main menu</u>.

At any time after reaching the <u>main menu</u> and before finishing a <u>transaction</u> (including before selecting a <u>transaction</u>), the <u>user</u> may press the <u>Cancel key</u>. The <u>transaction</u> being specified (if there is one) is canceled, the <u>user</u>'s <u>card</u> is returned, the <u>receipt of all transactions</u> is printed, and the <u>machine</u> once again becomes idle.

If a <u>deposit transaction</u> is selected, the <u>user</u> is asked to specify the <u>account</u> to which <u>funds</u> are to be deposited and the <u>amount</u> of the <u>deposit</u>, and to insert a <u>deposit envelope</u>.

If a <u>withdrawal transaction</u> is selected, the <u>user</u> is asked to specify the <u>account</u> from which <u>funds</u> are to be withdrawn and the <u>amount</u> of the <u>withdrawal</u>. If the <u>account</u> contains <u>sufficient funds</u>, the <u>funds</u> are given to the <u>user</u> through the <u>cash dispenser</u>.

If a <u>transfer of funds</u> is selected, the <u>user</u> is asked to specify the <u>account</u> from which the <u>funds</u> are to be withdrawn, the <u>account</u> to which the <u>funds</u> are to be deposited, and the <u>amount</u> of the <u>transfer</u>. If <u>sufficient funds</u> exist, the <u>transfer</u> is made.

If a balance inquiry is selected, the user is asked to specify the account whose balance is requested. The balance is not displayed, but is printed on the receipt.

Listing the Nouns

From the preceding specification, we get the following list of nouns. (Note that this is a complete, unedited list. We'll refine it as we go along.)

Automated Teller Machine	Deposit drawer	Funds
ATM	Cancel key	Balance
Machine	Greeting message	Information
Bank customer	Key	System
Financial transaction	Bank card	Feedback
Display screen	Card	Receipt
Bank card reader	User	Deposit transaction
Numeric input key	Personal Identification Number	Amount
Special input key	PIN	Deposit
Money dispenser slot	Digit	Deposit envelope
Deposit slot	Numeric keypad	Withdrawal transaction
Receipt printer	Main menu	Withdrawal
Element	Authorized bank employee	Transfer of funds
Special keypad	List of transactions	Transfer
Normal keypad	Account	Sufficient funds
Cash dispenser	Printer	Balance inquiry
Chances	Failure	Transaction
Third try		

The Elimination Phase

Obviously the preceding list of nouns needs some refinement. In this section, we'll refine the list of nouns into a list of possible classes.

Step 1: Making Nouns Understandable

The most basic step is to replace some nouns with other, more understandable phrases. Here are the nouns that will be replaced, with their replacements in parentheses:

Automated Teller Machine (ATM)	Money dispenser slot (Cash dispenser)
Card (Bank Card)	Normal keypad (Numeric keypad)
Deposit (Deposit transaction)	Personal Identification Number (PIN)
Deposit drawer (Deposit slot)	Printer (Receipt printer)
Digit (Numeric input key)	Sufficient funds (Balance)
Financial transaction (Transaction)	System (ATM)
Funds (Balance)	Transfer (Funds transfer)
Machine (ATM)	Withdrawal (Withdrawal transaction)

You may notice that this list also combines duplicate nouns that refer to the same real-world entity, such as Automated Teller Machine and ATM.

Step 2: Eliminating Outside Entities

Next, we eliminate anything that is outside the ATM system. Although the large bank system may have to deal with these outside entities, they're not necessary in our software model of an ATM:

Authorized bank employee	Receipt
Bank card	Time
Bank customer	User
Deposit envelope	

Step 3: Comparing to the Requirements

Now that we've eliminated the nouns that are obviously not part of our system, let's compare the remaining ones to the initial requirements specification.

The two nouns Greeting message and Main menu are very specific. Although they were mentioned in the original specification, it's reasonable to assume that the ATM deals with more than one kind of message and, possibly, more than one kind of menu. Given this, it makes sense to replace Greeting message and Main menu with the more generic Message and Menu.

The List of transactions mentioned in the specification is difficult: it implies some kind of transaction log, yet none was requested anywhere else in the specification. This point will need to be clarified with the user in a future design meeting. For now, we'll assume that a transaction log is not part of the ATM system design.

The noun Element is so generic as to be virtually worthless. However, if we look back at the specification, we can see that it refers to the physical elements of the ATM machine. Because it will probably be useful to group these things together, we'll keep this class. However, we'll rename it to something more understandable, such as Device.

Information is another vague-sounding term. It's unclear exactly what information is meant by this term, so for now, we'll discard it.

The Final List

Here's how our list looks now:

Account	Device	Receipt printer
ATM	Display screen	Special input key
Balance inquiry	Funds transfer	Special keypad
Bank card reader	Key	Transaction
Cancel key	Menu	User message
Cash dispenser	Numeric input key	Withdrawal transaction
Deposit slot	Numeric keypad	
Deposit transaction	PIN	

Defining the Responsibilities

Now it's time to go down the list of nouns and list the responsibilities for each one. At this point, it's often helpful to have a stack of CRC cards ready. Write the name of the class (because that is what the nouns are about to become) at the top of the card. Here are the responsibilities of each of our candidate classes:

Account

• Know the account balance

• Accept withdrawals

• Accept deposits

ATM

- Create and initiate transactions
- Display messages
- Display menus

Balance Inquiry

- Know how to cancel itself
- Prompt for the account whose balance is sought

Bank Card Reader

- Read bank cards
- Inform user of unreadable cards
- Eject bank cards
- Prompt the user for a PIN
- Keep bank cards whose PIN is not correctly entered

Cancel Key

- Know when it has been pressed
- Reset itself

Cash Dispenser

- Dispense funds to the user

Deposit Slot

- Accept a deposit envelope

Deposit Transaction

- Know how to cancel itself

- Prompt for the account in which to deposit funds

- Prompt for the amount to be deposited

Device

- No responsibilities

Display Screen

- Display text and graphics

Funds Transfer

- Know how to cancel itself

- Prompt for the account from which to withdraw funds

- Prompt for the account in which to deposit funds

- Prompt for the amount to be transferred

- Transfer funds

Key

- Know when it has been pressed

Menu

- Present the user with a list of choices

- Know if the user has responded

- Know the user's response

Numeric Input Key

- Know it has been pressed

Numeric Keypad

- Know which keys have been pressed

PIN

- No responsibilities

Receipt Printer

- Print receipt of transactions

Special Input Key

- Know it has been pressed

Special Keypad

- Know which keys have been pressed

Transaction

- Know how to cancel itself

Message

- Display message text

Withdrawal Transaction

- Know how to cancel itself

- Prompt for the account from which to withdraw funds

- Prompt for the amount to be withdrawn

Finding the Classes

No, we're not completely skipping the "Defining the Attributes" step. But the complete list is too extensive to show here, and is not really needed in order to begin grouping our cards.

The "Key Classes"

The first thing we notice from the preceding list is that the Key cards all have a responsibility in common, namely "Know it has been pressed." If we eliminate this responsibility from all the specific cards, leave it on the Key card, and make all the other key cards into subclasses, we get a class hierarchy that looks like that shown in Figure 7–10.

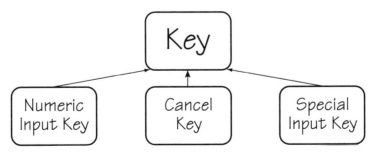

Figure 7–10. *The Key Classes.*

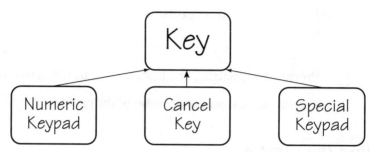

Figure 7–11. *The new Key classes.*

However, now the Cancel Key card is the only one that has any responsibilities other than those it inherits from Key. In fact, if we look at the list again, we notice that Numeric Keypad and Special Keypad have the responsibility "Know which keys have been pressed." Because this pretty much encompasses the behaviors of the individual keys, we can eliminate the individual key classes and make Cancel Key a special kind of keypad. Now our hierarchy looks like that shown in Figure 7–11.

The "Transaction" Classes

Next we notice that the "Know how to cancel itself" responsibility is shared by the Balance Inquiry, Deposit Transaction, Funds Transfer, Withdrawal Transaction and Transaction cards. Because Transaction is the most generic of these, we can make the other classes into subclasses of Transaction and eliminate the duplicate responsibilities. This gives us the hierarchy shown in Figure 7–12.

The "Device" Class

Although the Device card has no responsibilities, it's useful as an abstract class under which we can group all the cards that

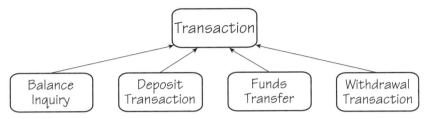

Figure 7–12. *The Transaction classes.*

relate to the physical ATM machine. These cards are as follows:

ATM	Cash dispenser	Numeric keypad
Bank card reader	Deposit slot	Receipt printer
Cancel key	Display screen	Special keypad

You may notice that these cards seem to be split into two rough groups: those that get things from the user, and those that give things to the user. We'll call these our Input Devices and our Output Devices. This leads us to the class tree shown in Figure 7–13.

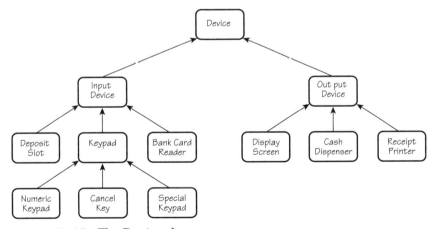

Figure 7–13. *The Device classes.*

Don't worry that we have two separate class hierarchies here. The two hierarchies may come together as we refine our design. Even if they don't, it's not essential that all class trees originate from a single parent.

Object-Oriented Design Notations

I mentioned earlier that once you've created your CRC cards and started to figure out the relationships between your classes, it's time to diagram your work. This brings up an interesting question: Which notation should you use?

There are many notations for diagramming object-oriented designs. There's the Booch-Rumbaugh notation, Wirfs-Brock, Jacobson, and so on. Each of them uses different symbols to represent classes, objects, and relationships, and each supports a slightly different development methodology. However, they all support some fundamental diagrams such as the Class Diagram. The ATM example in the previous section showed some examples of class diagrams.

An exhaustive discussion of the different design methodologies and notations is beyond the scope of this book. However, several books on the subject are available, both from independent authors and from the Object Management Group (OMG). The most important thing is not which methodology or notation you use, but that everyone in the team uses the same one. Evaluate the options carefully and pick the one that suits your company. You can even pick pieces from different methodologies and create a scheme that's unique to your company.

Design Patterns

Once you have some experience with object-oriented design, you may notice that certain designs appear again and again in different applications. This is known as a *design pattern*—a description of a set of classes that can be used to solve a similar problem in many different systems.

Design patterns are useful time-saving devices, and you should document them whenever you find them. However, you can learn from the combined experience of many object-oriented designers by buying one of the available design pattern books. Probably the most famous book on the subject is *Design Patterns: Elements of Reusable Object-Oriented Software* by Erich Gamma, Richard Helm, Ralph Johnson, and John Vlissides. More information on this book can be found in Appendix B.

General Design Tips

As a general rule, the first few object-oriented designs you do will take the longest, partly because of inexperience and partly because you don't have an existing library of designs from which to draw. The tips in this section prevent you from making some common design mistakes.

Don't Normalize Classes

Most of us have been designing database applications for a long time, and the most common trap we fall into is to normalize class designs. However, normalization is used to make disk usage more efficient and therefore reduce query times. Because objects are memory entities, this is less of an issue.

Your class designs should mimic the real world. For example, let's say I'm writing a student registration system for a school. In the real world, there are students and courses. Each student knows which courses they've registered for, and we can look at each course to see a list of registered students. When creating a class design, I would design a Student class that had an array of Course objects as one of its properties and a Course class that contained an array of Student objects.

If I were designing a data structure for this example, I would need a Students table, a Courses table, and a Students-Courses table. However, there's no such thing in the real world as a Student-Course. Because we can store the same information in the Student and Course classes, there's no need for the intermediate step.

Imagine your classes as "windows" onto underlying tables. Your data design should be efficient and normalized, but multiple classes may provide access to that data.

Decide When to Inherit

Earlier, I said that inheritance is used when one class is a "kind of" another class. The decision of when to subclass can be a little confusing, especially to those of us who are accustomed to dealing with databases. If you find yourself including properties such as IDs or logical flags, look carefully to see whether inheritance would be a better solution. Here are some general rules:

- Use a logical flag if you just need to know what kind of entity you're dealing with.

- Use inheritance if the behaviors and attributes can vary depending on the type of entity.

For example, in a Rolodex system, it would be useful to know which contacts are new and have never been called. This would best be stored in a logical flag. However, the actions taken and the data stored may be different, depending on whether the contact is a business contact or a personal friend, so it would be best to create an abstract Contact class with two subclasses for business and personal contacts.

Don't Skip Business Analysis

When analyzing a company's current processes, many developers concern themselves only with the processes associated with their particular application. However, it can be very helpful to have an overall understanding of the business as a whole. After all, the classes you create now aren't going to be used in just this application; instead, they'll be used again and again in different systems for this company. Obviously this means that the class designs must be appropriate for the company, rather than for a particular application.

During the initial "brainstorming" design sessions, it can be very helpful to involve a representative from the client in the discussions. At this early stage, most of the questions you'll have will be about the business rather than about computer entities such as data structures. No one can answer these questions better than your client, and early involvement not only ensures your understanding of the business, but also makes the client feel a part of the process rather than a passive observer.

Think of the Future

One of the first questions every developer should ask a client is: What are your future plans for automation? How can you develop a system that meets the client's needs for the next few years if you don't know exactly what those needs are? Writing an application to a rigid specification may give clients what they asked for, but not necessarily what they need.

When designing classes for a system, keep in mind the possible future uses of those classes. It may be worth the effort to add some functionality that isn't needed for this particular system, but will be used in the future. For example, in the insurance system mentioned earlier, I put some properties and methods into the Policy class that weren't needed by the system I was writing at that time. However, because the real-world policy didn't change, I was able to use the Policy class (the software representation of that real-world policy) in many other applications without having to change it later.

Remember that we're not writing any code at the moment: we're working on design only. You may choose to add functionality to the design that you don't implement until later releases, but by adding it to the design now, you've ensured that there's a place to put that functionality when it's needed.

Work as Part of a Team

If you have the luxury of working as part of a development team, take advantage of it. Having other experienced developers pick apart your class designs can illustrate shortcomings far earlier than you might notice them on your own.

If you work alone, try to find other developers who can be bribed with dinner in exchange for critiquing your designs! Or start a study group with other developers in your area or over CompuServe or the Internet. If you belong to a user group, consider starting a design workshop before the main meeting and looking at one person's design each month. Whichever avenue you choose, try to find other developers to work with. It will eventually save you a lot of time.

Processes Can Be Classes, Too

The most obvious classes are those that represent real-world entities like policies and customers. However, some complex processes may be good candidates for class creation. Here are the general clues that indicate that a process should be made into a class:

- The process has several stages, each of which can be started, stopped, and rolled back.

- State information is stored as each stage completes. For example, you may need to store the name of the person completing each stage, the date, and so on.

Earlier in this chapter, we looked at an ATM example that included classes for the various transactions that an ATM can perform. These are good examples of processes that are implemented as classes.

Summary

Object-oriented analysis and design is a very detailed topic, and we've only scratched the surface in this chapter. Although I've tried to give an overview of the basic techniques, I recommend reading the design books mentioned in Appendix B.

Chapter 8 looks at the typical roles found in an object-oriented design team and the problems they face.

8

The Object-Oriented Development Team

Nowadays, most applications are too large to be designed, developed, and tested by individual programmers. In many corporations, programmers work as part of a team responsible for automating the corporation's processes. Working as part of a team has many benefits. However, although it's often useful to look at a problem from another point of view before writing a solution, team development has its own set of problems.

This chapter looks at the most common roles in an object-oriented development team and the development standards that must be agreed upon for the team to function effectively.

Personalities in the Team

In a company that uses object technology, a development team is usually broken down into five basic roles:

1. Class Designer

2. Class Implementor

3. Application Designer/Implementor

4. Team Coordinator

5. Reuse Librarian

As client/server applications become more and more popular, many companies are adding a sixth role: the Business Rule Designer. This is the person who decides on the business rules (for example, "A part price can never be a negative number") that will eventually be translated into rules and triggers in the database engine.

In smaller companies, some roles (such as Class Designer and Class Implementor) may be combined. It doesn't really matter whether each person is filling one role or several; what's important is that all the roles are recognized and fulfilled. So let's take a more detailed look at the five roles.

Class Designer

A Class Designer is someone who considers the best way to represent a real-world entity—such as a Customer—in software. The Class Designer is not concerned with issues such as data structures or screen design, but concentrates on the responsibilities and attributes of each class. Some people find it easier than others to focus solely on design while ignoring implementation issues. These people are good candidates for the role of Class Designer. (See Figure 8–1.)

The work done by the Class Designer is very important because it will be the foundation of other classes that will be created in the future. If you're working in this role, pay careful attention to the placement of responsibilities and the relationships between your classes because these are difficult to change later. Keep any CRC cards that you use to develop a design because they will be useful memory-joggers in the future.

The Class Designer is responsible not only for the structure of each class, but also for the public interface. If you recall from

Figure 8–1. *The Class Designer.*

the discussion of scoping in Chapter 4, the public interface consists of the exported properties and methods in the class definition. The Class Designer's contribution to this interface deals primarily with the attributes defined in the initial design discussions. Properties and methods that are added during implementation are the responsibility of the Class Implementor.

 TIP: To take advantage of the power of polymorphism, it's important that the same name be used to refer to similar items.

Class Implementor

Once a class has been designed, it must be turned over to the Class Implementor to be constructed in code. In smaller development teams, the Class Designer and Class Implementor are often the same person; however, we'll look at them separately because they are different roles.

When designing a class, the Class Designer tries to give as little thought as possible to implementation details. Although the Class Implementor tries to follow the design as closely as possible, some changes may have to be made due to implementation considerations. For example, a class may prove too slow using the recommended structure. When situations like this occur, the Class Implementor works with the Class Designer to revise the design. (See Figure 8–2.)

In some cases, the Class Implementor may be able to suggest ways to improve the usability of a class or an individual method. This change should be suggested to the Class Designer rather than implemented directly by the Implementor, so that the change fits in with the rest of the classes currently under design.

The Class Implementor may also have to add properties and methods to a class in order to implement successfully. These tend to be computer properties such as flags and nonbusiness methods such as Print and Save.

Application Designer/Implementor

The Application Designer/Implementor is often the more junior person on the development team. (See Figure 8–3.) The person filling this role must take the classes that have been designed

Figure 8–2. *The Class Implementor.*

and implemented and add the necessary menus, screens, and "glue" code to create a working application.

It's very helpful if the Application Designer has extensive knowledge of the *problem domain*, that is, the business area being modeled. A person with expertise in the problem domain is called a *domain expert*.

The Team Coordinator, aka the "Referee"

The Team Coordinator has the job of mediating between the other members of the development team to come up with a sys-

"APPLICATION DESIGNER/IMPLEMENTOR"

Figure 8–3. *The Application Designer/Implementor.*

tem that meets the client's needs. However, the Team Coordinator must also keep in mind the long-term needs of the development company. Some tough questions must be answered, such as:

- Will this change result in future business, or will it hinder the use of these classes in other applications for other clients?

- Will the addition of this class to a design make it easier to extend the system in the future, or is it unnecessary overhead?

TIP: The Team Coordinator must be a person with sufficient proficiency in object technology to make these decisions. However, they must also *have the authority* to make a decision by which the other team members must abide.

In addition to the needs of the client, the Team Coordinator must also be aware of the long-term implications of a solution. For example, as the Application Designer/Implementor begins to use a set of classes to create an application, a deficiency is noticed. The problem could be solved either by asking the Class Designer to redesign the appropriate classes to solve the deficiency, or by asking the Application Designer/Implementor to work around the deficiency in the name of expediency. The Team Coordinator must consider the long-term needs of the team: will this deficiency be a problem again in the future with another application, or is this an unusual circumstance? (See Figure 8–4.)

Reuse Librarian

In many environments, the person who does the analysis and design of a system is also the person who writes that system. Any generic functions that are developed as a result of that effort are added to the company library. It is unusual for a company to specifically assign someone to maintain the company function library. This is not the case in a company using object

"TEAM COORDINATOR"

Figure 8–4. *The Team Coordinator.*

technology, where the Reuse Librarian is an important team member. (See Figure 8–5.)

The Reuse Librarian's job is to examine every class to see if it fits in with the company's existing class libraries. The Reuse Librarian typically works with the Class Designers from the beginning. Although reuse is touted as one of the benefits of object orientation, it can only be achieved with planning.

Figure 8–5. *The Reuse Librarian.*

The role of Reuse Librarian becomes more important when you consider the idea of software metrics. In an object-oriented development project, measuring programmer productivity by lines of code produced is pointless. What we're trying to reward is solution production, rather than code-churning. Increasingly, companies are rewarding the amount of code *reuse* that occurs, rather than code production.

Coding Conventions

Coding conventions are especially important in a multiprogrammer environment. They ensure that code can be easily and quickly read and understood by other team members, even after the original programmer has left the team. Coding conventions are also important when bringing in new team members because they reduce the amount of time it takes for the new members to understand the existing code. In this section, we'll look at a couple of suggestions that make it easier to share code in a team environment.

Hungarian Notation

Visual FoxPro (like most other Xbase dialects) does not support *strong typing* of memory variables and properties. A strongly typed language allows you to specify the data (or object) type of a variable or property when it is created. For example, in the following line:

```
LOCAL custNum
```

it isn't clear what kind of data custNum contains. Compare this with the same line written in a strongly typed language, and you can see how the second example removes any ambiguity:

```
LOCAL custNum AS Int
```

In addition to being more understandable, this code is also faster, because the compiler can tell custNum's data type and can therefore hard-wire it to mathematical operations. There is also no possibility that custNum will "accidentally" change type in another routine; it must always be an integer.

Although it isn't possible in Visual FoxPro to achieve the speed benefits of a strongly typed language, it is possible to resolve data type ambiguity with *Hungarian notation*. Using this notation, a lowercase letter or group of letters is added to the beginning of the variable or property name to represent the data type.

These prefixes (sometimes called *metasymbols*) can be expanded to include the scope of the property or variable.

Tables 8–1, 8–2, and 8–3 show the Hungarian notation used for objects and memory variables in Visual FoxPro. This information was taken from the *Visual FoxPro 3.0 Codebook*, and used as a basis for the conventions developed by Microsoft. For objects, a three-character prefix is used to show the object type. You'll have to define the characters used for your company-standard classes.

Table 8–1. *Object Prefixes*

Object	Prefix	Example
Check box	chk	chkReadOnly
Combo box	cbo	cboEnglish
Command button	cmd	cmdCancel
Container	cnt	cntCustomerInfo
Control	ctl	ctlMisc
Edit Box	edt	edtComments
Form	frm	frmFileOpen
Form page	fpg	fpgList
Form set	frs	frsCustomerInfo
Grid	grd	grdPrices
Grid column	grc	grcCompanyName
Grid header	grh	grhLineTotal
Image	img	imgIcon
Label	lbl	lblHelpMessage
Line	lin	linVertical
List box	lst	lstPolicyCodes
OLE	ole	oleObject1

Table 8-1. *Object Prefixes* *(continued)*

Object	Prefix	Example
Option button	opt	optFrench
Option group	opg	opgType
Outline control	otl	otlViews
Page frame	pgf	pgfLeft
Shape (circle, square, oval, rectangle, rounded rectangle, and rounded square)	shp	shpCircle
Spinner	spn	spnDaysShown
Text box	txt	txtGetText
Timer	tmr	tmrAlarm
Toolbar	tbr	tbrEditReport

Table from Griver's *The Visual FoxPro 3.0 Codebook* (see Appendix B).

For memory variables, two prefixes are used. The first represents the variable's scope, and the second indicates its type. These type prefixes are also used for object properties.

Table 8-2. *Memory Variable Scope Prefixes*

Scope	Prefix	Example
Public/Global	g	gcUserName
Private	p	pcState
Local	l	lnCounter
Parameter	t	tdRun
Class	<none>	Customer
Constant (#DEFINE)	ALLCAPS	TRUE

Table 8–3. *Memory Variable/Property Type Prefixes*

Type	Prefix	Example
Character	c	cLastName
Numeric	n	nRangeLo
Logical	l	lMarried
Date	d	dPurchased
Memo	m	mComments
General	g	gWordDoc
Currency	y	ySalary
Float	f	fResults
Double	b	bValue
Picture	p	pEmployee
DateTime	t	tRecorded
Object Instance	o	oJanitor
Array	a	aMonths

One Argument Against Hungarian Notation

Although most developers agree that Hungarian notation is valuable for procedural code, some suggest that it is contrary to the encapsulation principle to adopt it for object-oriented code. They say that prefacing a property with a letter denoting its data type reveals too much information about the internal implementation of the property. However, it is safe to say that Hungarian notation is a reasonable choice, given that the name of an exported property is part of the public interface to the class.

Traditional object-oriented languages such as Smalltalk generally do not use Hungarian notation for properties. However, this is an issue that you will need to decide for yourselves, with the help of the Team Coordinator.

Naming Conventions

Another major standard that must be decided is that of property and method naming. It's very important that you follow a consistent naming convention throughout your classes, or it will be difficult to realize the benefits of polymorphism. There's no benefit to being able to send the same message to different kinds of object if you've used different method names for each class.

I recommend that you follow the conventions used in Visual FoxPro. For example, most visual classes use a Show method to display themselves, so it's a good idea to use "Show" as the method name whenever you need to display information.

Careful consideration of naming conventions can also make it easier for programmers with experience in other object-oriented languages to make the transition into your team. For example, Visual FoxPro uses the CreateObject() function to create new instances of a class. However, many other object-oriented languages use the New message. By avoiding the use of "New" as a method name in your classes, you will avoid confusing non-FoxPro programmers.

Summary

For those of you who work in teams for application development, this chapter provided an overview of typical team roles. However, not all of us are fortunate enough to have other designers to bounce ideas off. If you work alone and have to fulfill all the roles outlined in this chapter, try to keep in mind which role you're playing at any point in time and remember the responsibilities of that role. If you can, persuade some fellow consultants to pick apart your class design. Or take your design to a user group and start a "Design Analysis" session before the regular meeting. I can almost guarantee that someone will point out a bad idea or two and possibly save you a great deal of time.

Now that you've read and (I hope!) understood the major terms and concepts involved in object-oriented design and programming, it's time to "go forth and objectify"! This book is just a start—you can learn a lot from other books and magazines on object orientation, whether or not they were written with Visual FoxPro in mind. Above all, remember that object orientation is just a programming paradigm, not a religion. There are pros and there are cons, and it's up to us as developers to find the balance.

Glossary of Terms

abstract class

A class that has no instances. An abstract class is created only for the purpose of organizing a class hierarchy or for defining methods and properties that will apply to lower level classes. The term "virtual class" is sometimes used to refer to the same concept.

abstract data type

A data type that is defined by the programmer and not built into the language. Abstract data types are typically used to create high-level structures that correspond to real-world objects represented in a program.

abstraction

The process of focusing on the essential characteristics of a class. Also known as generalization. *See also* abstract class.

access method

A method that is called whenever a property is accessed. Not currently supported in Visual FoxPro.

actor

A set of roles that an entity can play in a system. Popularized by Ivar Jacobson. Grady Booch additionally defines an actor as "an object that can operate upon other objects but is never operated upon by other objects." *See also* agent.

agent

An object that can both operate on other objects and be operated on by other objects. *See also* actor.

aggregate class

A class that contains one or more objects of other classes. Another term for a composite or container class.

aggregation

The process of creating a class that is made up in whole or in part of objects of other classes. *See also* aggregate class.

application framework

A set of classes that define methods and properties for a generic application, which can then be subclassed to tailor the application for a specific purpose. *See also* framework.

assign method

A method that is called whenever a property has a value assigned to it. Assign methods allow you to easily validate the value being assigned. Not currently supported in Visual FoxPro.

base class

The most generalized class in a class structure, from which other classes are created. Most applications have many such base classes. Some languages define a primitive base class that serves as the ultimate superclass of all classes. *Note:* Visual FoxPro uses the term "base class" to refer to the classes that are built into the product.

binding

The process of weaving a program together to resolve all the connections among its components. Early binding resolves these connections before the program is run. Late binding occurs while the program is running.

browser

A tool for viewing and debugging classes or objects. Visual FoxPro comes with a Class Browser that can also display objects.

calculated property

A property that does not actually exist but is calculated each time its value is accessed. Because Visual FoxPro does not yet support access and assign methods, calculated properties cannot yet be supported. *See also* access method.

cardinality

The number of instances that a class may have; the number of instances that participate in a using class relationship.

child class

See subclass.

child control

A control that is part of a form object or class. Unlike a child class, a child control has no inheritance relationship with its parent.

class

A template that defines the methods and properties for a particular type of object; a set of objects that share a common behavior.

class diagram

Part of the notation of object-oriented design, used to show the existence of classes and their relationships in the logical design of a system.

class hierarchy

A tree structure representing the relationships among a set of classes. Class hierarchies usually have one top node but may have any number of levels in the tree and any number of classes at each level.

class library

A collection of generic classes that can be adapted and tailored for a particular application.

class method

A method invoked by sending a message to a class rather than to one of its instances. Class methods usually perform tasks that cannot or should not be performed at the instance level. For example, creating and destroying instances of a class is something that cannot be done by the instances themselves. Not currently supported in Visual FoxPro.

class property

A placeholder for part of the state of a class. Collectively the class properties of a class constitute its structure. A class property is shared by all instances of that class. Not currently supported in Visual FoxPro.

collaboration

The process of working with an object of another class in order to accomplish a task. Collaboration usually implies a using or an is-part-of relationship.

composite class

A class that contains one or more other objects by storing references to those objects in its properties. Also known in Visual FoxPro as a container class.

constructor

A method that creates an object and/or initializes its state. In Visual FoxPro, the constructor is the code between the DEFINE CLASS statement and the first method.

container class

See composite class.

contract

An "agreement" that sets out the responsibilities that two classes will provide to one another.

CRC card

Class-Responsibility-Collaborator card. An index card on which are written the class name, its responsibilities, its collaborators, and (optionally) its attributes. CRC cards are usually 3x5 or 5x7 index cards.

derived class

See subclass.

design pattern

A reusable design for a set of classes to solve a particular kind of generic problem.

destructor

An operation that frees the state of an object and/or destroys the object itself.

domain expert

A person with specialized knowledge of the problem domain being modeled. Often an outside consultant or a representative from the client company.

early binding

See binding.

encapsulation

The bundling, within a class, of data (properties) and the code (methods) that operate on that data. Access to the data is permitted only through the object's own methods. The terms "encapsulation" and "information hiding" are usually interchangeable.

event-driven

An event-driven system dispatches events (user actions and system events) to the application, allowing the user navigational control of the interface with the underlying program ready to respond whenever action is appropriate.

event method

A method that is triggered automatically in response to an event occurring in the system. In Visual FoxPro, an event method always has the same name as the corresponding event.

framework

A detailed set of classes aimed at a particular business area. *See also* application framework.

friend class/function

A class or function that has access to the protected or hidden properties and methods of another class, even though it is not a part of and does not inherit from the other class. Originated in C++. Not currently supported in Visual FoxPro.

generalization

See abstraction.

hierarchy

A ranking or ordering of abstractions. The two most common hierarchies in a complex system are its class structure (the "kind of" hierarchy) and its object structure (the "part of" hierarchy). *See also* class hierarchy.

identity

A distinguishing characteristic of an object that denotes a separate existence of the object, even though the object may have the same data values as another object.

inheritance

A mechanism whereby a class can make use of the methods and properties defined in all classes above it on its branch (single inheritance) and/or other branches (multiple inheritance) of the class hierarchy.

initializer

A method whose purpose is to set the initial values of properties. In Visual FoxPro, the initializer is always called Init. In some languages, the initialization code is placed inside the constructor.

instance

An object created from a class. A class defines the structure of its instances; the class thereby acts as a "factory" for the creation of instances.

instance variable

A variable contained within an object, whose value describes properties that the object possesses. *Note:* Visual FoxPro uses the term "property" instead of "instance variable."

instantiation

The process of creating instances from classes. This is done with the CreateObject() function in Visual FoxPro.

late binding

See binding.

manager class

A class whose purpose is to manage instances of other classes. Examples are WindowManager and CustomerManager. Manager classes typically contain methods that act on all instances of a class.

member access operator

The operator that appears between the object name and the message name when sending a message to an object. Also known as the send operator or dot operator. In Visual FoxPro, the member access operator is a period (.).

member object

An object that is stored in a property of another class. Also known as an object member.

message

A signal from one object to another, requesting that the receiving object carry out one of its methods. A message consists of three parts: the name of the receiver, the method it is to carry out (or property to access), and any parameters the method may require in order to fulfill its duty.

metaclass

A class whose instances are themselves classes. Not currently supported in Visual FoxPro.

method

The function or procedure that responds to a message sent by another object. Methods determine how an object will respond to a message it receives.

multiple inheritance

A type of inheritance that permits a class to have more than one superclass. The use of multiple inheritance complicates the structure of the class hierarchy but can sometimes provide more flexibility for defining classes. Not currently supported in Visual FoxPro. *See also* inheritance.

name clashing

A conflict that can occur in multiple inheritance, when the same method or property is inherited from more than one class.

object

A software package containing a collection of related data and methods for operating on that data.

object database

A database in which objects can be saved in their entirety without being broken down into individual tables.

operator overloading

The ability to use standard operators like + and - to conduct mathematical operations on objects. A form of polymorphism for operators. Not currently supported in Visual FoxPro.

parent class

See superclass.

parent form

The form on which child controls appear. This does not imply an inheritance relationship and is different than a parent class.

persistence

The permanence of an object's state and relationships.

polymorphism

The ability of the same message to be interpreted differently when received by different objects. For example, the message Print causes a different series of actions when sent to a diagram than when sent to a text document.

problem domain

The business area being modeled.

process diagram

Part of the notation of object-oriented design, used to show the allocation of processes to processors in the physical design of a system.

property

Another name for an instance variable.

rapid prototyping

A technique of software development in which a program is developed incrementally as a series of "trial versions" that gradually converge on the desired functionality. Rapid prototyping differs from traditional prototyping because the prototype is not thrown away but is refined into the deliverable system.

receiver

The object to which a message is sent. A sender object passes a message to the receiver object, which processes the message and optionally passes back a return value.

self

Used in methods to refer to the object currently being acted upon. Referred to in Visual FoxPro as this.

sender

The object initiating a message.

single inheritance

A type of inheritance in which each class may have only one superclass. *See also* inheritance.

state

The values of the attributes of an object at a particular time.

state transition diagram

A diagram that shows the events that cause an object's transition from one state to another, and the actions that result from that state change.

subclass

A class that refines or overrides behaviors of its superclass(es). A subclass appears below its superclass(es) in the class hierarchy. *Note:* Visual FoxPro sometimes uses the term "child class" to refer to a subclass.

superclass

A more abstract version of another class (the subclass). A superclass appears above its subclasses in the class hierarchy. *Note:* Visual FoxPro uses the term "parent class" to refer to a superclass.

this

Used in methods to refer to the object currently being acted upon. Referred to in some languages as self.

transition

A change of state caused by an event.

use

A relationship in which a class manipulates or makes visible the attributes and behaviors of another class.

use case

A sequence of business steps that can be used to evaluate the robustness and accuracy of a class design.

wrapper class

A class whose purpose is to provide an object-oriented interface to an older, typically procedural piece of code.

Bibliography

Booch, Grady. *Object–Oriented Design with Applications.*
Redwood City, CA: Benjamin/Cummings, 1991, ISBN 0-8053-0091-0

> Provides a comprehensive description of object-oriented design
> methods, using the popular Booch notation. Also includes five
> real-world application designs, each implemented in a different
> language. Languages covered are Smalltalk, Object Pascal, C++,
> CLOS, and Ada.

Brentnall, Savannah, Ellen Sander, and John Gunn. *The Visual
Guide to Visual FoxPro.* **Research Triangle Park, NC: Ventana,
1995, ISBN 1-56604-227-5**

> OK, so I'm biased! This book is aimed at beginning to intermedi-
> ate FoxPro developers, not end users. It covers all the new fea-
> tures of Visual FoxPro and includes extensive coverage of the
> object model. Does not assume previous FoxPro knowledge.

Gamma, Erich, Richard Helm, Ralph Johnson, and John Vlissides.
Design Patterns. **Reading, MA: Addison-Wesley, 1995,
ISBN 0-201-63361-2**

> Contains a series of object-oriented designs that are aimed at
> practicing O-O professionals. This book doesn't explain how to
> design object-oriented applications; rather, it provides a set of

proven designs for typical problems. These designs can be implemented in almost any object-oriented language, including Visual FoxPro.

Griver, Y. Alan. *The Visual FoxPro 3.0 Codebook.* Alameda, CA: Sybex, 1995, ISBN 0-7821-1648-5

The *FoxPro 2.6 Codebook* was one of the best-selling FoxPro books around, and its author is a well-known speaker and industry figure. The Visual FoxPro version isn't a guide to the features of the product; instead, it provides guidelines on how best to use those features. The *Codebook* discusses business reengineering and the ways in which it can be supported by the Visual FoxPro object model.

Jacobson, Ivar. *The Object Advantage: Business Process Reengineering with Object Technology.* Reading, MA: Addison-Wesley, 1994, ISBN 0-201-42289-1

Describes how to apply the author's well-known object-oriented design methodology to business process reengineering. This book focuses specifically on the Jacobson methodology, in contrast with David Taylor's more generic business reengineering text. Easy to read and doesn't really require previous experience with the methodology.

Meyer, Bertrand. *Object-Oriented Software Construction.* Englewood Cliffs, NJ: Prentice Hall, 1988, ISBN 0-13-629049-3

An old favorite and still a useful reference. This book explains the idea of "programming by contract" and is the book on which much of Nantucket's material on modular programming was based. Source code examples are written in Eiffel.

Mullin, Mark. *Rapid Prototyping for Object–Oriented Systems.* **Reading, MA: Addison-Wesley, 1990, ISBN 0-201-55024-5**

> Explains the principles of this design methodology by walking the reader through the generation of an actual prototype. Discusses the needs of the client and client-program interaction, as well as actual system features. Language examples are in Smalltalk.

Pinson, Lewis J., and Richard S. Wiener. *An Introduction to Object–Oriented Programming and Smalltalk.* **Reading MA: Addison-Wesley, 1988, ISBN 0-201-19127**

> Explains the principles of object orientation in the context of the Smalltalk language. Covers Smalltalk classes, both fundamental and advanced.

Rumbaugh, James, Michael Blaha, William Premerlani, Frederick Eddy, and William Loerensen. *Object–Oriented Modeling and Design.* **Englewood Cliffs, NJ: Prentice Hall, 1991, ISBN 0-13-629841-9**

> Describes the authors' Object Modeling Technique notation. A somewhat academic tone, but includes three case studies.

Taylor, David A. *Business Engineering with Object Technology.* **New York, NY: Wiley,1995, ISBN 0-471-04521-7**

> Written in Taylor's usual easy-to-read style, this book explains how object technology can be used to aid in business reengineering projects. The book suggests that classes be created not for particular applications, but to model the business as a whole. A good introduction to a subject that is receiving more and more attention.

Taylor, David A. *Object-Oriented Information Systems.*
New York, NY: Wiley, 1992, ISBN 0-471-54364-0

> Clear and easy to read. Explains how to plan and implement
> object-oriented systems, and includes a series of real-world case
> studies.

Taylor, David A. *Object-Oriented Technology: A Manager's Guide.*
Reading, MA: Addison-Wesley, 1990, ISBN 0-201-56358-4

> A guide to object orientation for everyone from managers to
> developers. Very easy to read, with great illustrations. An ideal
> book for anyone looking for simple, clear explanations of basic
> concepts, and especially useful for those who have to convince
> others of the technology's merits.

Tkachk, Daniel, and Richard Puttick. *Object Technology in*
Application Development.
Redwood City, CA: Benjamin/Cummings, 1994, ISBN 0-8053-2572-7

> Developed at IBM's International Technical Support Center in
> San Jose, California. Covers the current state of object technol-
> ogy, including available object-oriented design notations, visual
> programming tools, team programming issues, and object data-
> bases. One of the few books to give an overview of the works of
> the various standards committees, such as the Object Manage-
> ment Group (OMG). Very easy to read.

Voss, Greg. *Object-Oriented Programming: An Introduction.*
Berkeley, CA: Osborne McGraw-Hill, 1991, ISBN 0-07-881682-3

> Introduces the core concepts of object-oriented programing and
> shows working examples in C++, Object Pascal, Actor, and
> Smalltalk.

White, Iseult. *Rational Rose Essentials: Using the Booch Method.*
Redwood City, CA: Benjamin/Cummings, 1994, ISBN 0-8053-0616-1

> Provides an easy reference for those interested in using the methodology and notation described in Grady Booch's *Object-Oriented Design with Applications*. Comes with a cut-down version of Rational Rose. Unfortunately the "cut-down" aspect refers to the inability to save class diagrams.

Winblad, Ann L., Samuel D. Edwards, and David R. King. *Object-Oriented Software.*
Reading, MA: Addison-Wesley, 1990, ISBN 0-201-50736-6

> Explains the key concepts and benefits of object-oriented technology. Gives a "big picture" view rather than concentrating on a particular language. Unlike other books, this one also discusses emerging methodologies and aspects of the technology that are still evolving.

Wirfs-Brock, Rebecca, Brian Wilkerson, and Lauren Wiener. *Designing Object-Oriented Software.*
Englewood Cliffs, NJ: Prentice-Hall, 1990, ISBN 0-13-629825-7

> An easy-to-read guide to object-oriented design, with extensive examples. Also covers the usc of CRC cards. Language-independent.

Index

Addison-Wesley Developers Press publishes high-quality, practical books and software for programmers, developers, and system administrators.

Here are some additional titles from A-W Developers Press that might interest you. If you'd like to order any of these books, you can use one of the following ordering methods:

FAX us at: 800-367-7198

Call us at: 800-822-6339
(8:30 A.M. to 6:00 P.M. eastern time, Monday through Friday)

Write to us at:
Addison-Wesley Developers Press
One Jacob Way
Reading, MA 01867

Reach us online at:
http://www.aw.com/devpress/

International orders, contact one of the following Addison-Wesley subsidiaries:

Australia/New Zealand
Addison-Wesley Publishing Co.
6 Byfield Street
North Ryde, N.S.W. 2113
Australia
Tel: 61 2 878 5411
Fax: 61 2 878 5830

Southeast Asia
Addison-Wesley
Singapore Pte. Ltd.
15 Beach Road
#05-09/10 Beach Centre
Singapore 189677
Tel: 65 339 7503
Fax: 65 338 6290

Latin America
Addison-Wesley Iberoamericana S.A.
Blvd. de las Cataratas #3
Col. Jardines del Pedregal
01900 Mexico D.F., Mexico
Tel: (52 5) 568-36-18
Fax: (52 5) 568-53-32
e-mail: ordenes@ibero.aw.com
 or: informaciona@ibero.aw.com

Europe and the Middle East
Addison-Wesley Publishers B.V.
Concertgebouwplein 25
1071 LM Amsterdam
The Netherlands
Tel: 31 20 671 7296
Fax: 31 20 675 2141

United Kingdom and Africa
Addison-Wesley Longman Group Limited
P.O. Box 77
Harlow, Essex CM 19 5BQ
United Kingdom
Tel: 44 1279 623 923
Fax: 44 1279 453 450

All other countries:
Addison-Wesley Publishing Co.
Attn: International Order Dept.
One Jacob Way
Reading, MA 01867 U.S.A.
Tel: (617) 944-3700 x5190
Fax: (617) 942-2829

If you'd like a free copy of our Developers Press catalog, contact us at: devpressinfo@aw.com

Hacker's Guide™ to Visual FoxPro® 3.0: An Irreverent Look at How FoxPro *Really* Works

Tamar E. Granor and Ted Roche
ISBN 0-201-48379-3, $44.95 w/disk

Hacker's Guide to Visual FoxPro 3.0 is the definitive reference to how all the commands, functions, properties, events, and methods in Visual FoxPro 3.0 *really* work. FoxPro experts Tamar Granor and Ted Roche show you which commands to use, which to avoid, and which ones don't work quite the way the manual says they do. You'll learn about common and not-so-common bugs and how to work around them, plus you get an introduction to OOP, SQL, and client/server, as well as productivity hints; tips for creating your own Builders and Wizards; and advanced coverage of OLE and OLE Automation.

Client/Server Technology for Managers

Karen Watterson
ISBN 0-201-40920-8, $17.95

Client/Server Technology for Managers concisely explains in nontechnical terms the uses, abuses, technology, and process of client/server computing. The book gives you a framework for decision making and explains the "big picture" of client/server computing, so that you can assess your company or organization's needs and opportunities and successfully employ this new technology to solve real-world professional challenges. *Client/Server Technology for Managers* will help you harness this very powerful but potentially confusing part of today's computing landscape.

The Practical SQL Handbook, Second Edition

Judith S. Bowman, Sandra L. Emerson and Marcy Darnovsky
ISBN 0-201-62623-3, $34.95

The Practical SQL Handbook is the best-selling guide to learning Structured Query Language (SQL), the standard language for accessing information in relational databases. This book teaches SQL not just as it has been established by ANSI standards committees, but as the language is used in the real world. This updated edition features two new chapters on implementing SQL in the workplace. These chapters are cookbooks of specific solutions, ready-to-use code, and general strategies for common business database challenges.